W9-AFF-042

WITHDRAWN

Manuel Puig

Twayne's World Authors Series

Latin American Literature

David William Foster, Editor
Arizona State University

TWAS 836

Manuel Puig
Photo © Jerry Bauer

Manuel Puig

Jonathan Tittler

Cornell University

Twayne Publishers ■ New York

Maxwell Macmillan Canada ■ Toronto

Maxwell Macmillan International ■ New York Oxford Singapore Sydney

Manuel Puig
Jonathan Tittler

Twayne Publishers   Maxwell Macmillan Canada, Inc.
Macmillan Publishing Company 1200 Eglinton Avenue East
866 Third Avenue   Suite 200
New York, New York 10022   Don Mills, Ontario M3C 3N1

Macmillan Publishing Company is part of the Maxwell Communications Group of Companies.

Library of Congress Cataloging-in-Publication Data

Tittler, Jonathan
    Manuel Puig / Jonathan Tittler.
    p. cm. – (Twayne's world authors series; TWAS 836)
    Includes bibliographical references and index.
    Summary: A critical study of the innovative Argentine's major writings, highlighted by a discussion of his personal life and career.
    ISBN 0-8057-8289-3
    1. Puig, Manuel – Criticism and interpretation. 2. Argentine literature – History and criticism I. Title. II. Series.
PQ7798.26.U4Z89 1993
863 – dc20   92-39794
                                                                        CIP
                                                                        AC

The paper used in this publication meets the minimum requirements of American National Standard for Information Sciences – Permanence of Paper for Printed Library Materials, ANSI Z39.48-1984.

10 9 8 7 6 5 4 3 2 1

Printed in the United States of America.

Contents

Preface

The Argentine author Manuel Puig (1932-90) looms today as a marginal figure of the much-commented "Boom" of the Latin American novel, and he wouldn't have had it any other way.[1] Widely recognized as an innovator of narrative technique, he was for many years mistakenly viewed as either a parodist of vulgar, mass-produced cultural products or a victim and purveyor of bad taste. Only recently has literary criticism come to put those elements together and to appreciate the depth of his ambivalence about melodrama and the extent of his commitment to subverting structures of authority, in whatever guise they might appear. This book, the first to appear since his untimely demise at the age of 57, while not claiming to establish a definitive assessment of his work, pretends at least to view it as a finite, though still shifting, whole. Rather than contend that Puig ought to be incorporated into the same central orbit as his more renowned contemporaries (principal among whom would be Julio Cortázar, José Donoso, Carlos Fuentes, Gabriel García Márquez, and Mario Vargas Llosa), I find it more appropriate to place him alongside such excellent but relatively unknown figures as the Cubans Guillermo Cabrera Infante, Severo Sarduy, and Reinaldo Arenas; the Chileans Antonio Skármeta and Ariel Dorfman; the Puerto Rican Luis Rafael Sánchez; or the Mexicans Vicente Leñero, Gustavo Sainz, and José Agustín. The last thing Manuel Puig would want – and I say this with a confidence derived from a decade of personal correspondence – is to be given the stature of a demigod.

The temptation to enshrine Puig remains, though. He is, after all, much more widely translated than any of the other "secondary" figures cited above. The broad dissemination of his works did translate during his life, moreover, into considerable financial success and artistic independence (only Nobel laureate García Márquez, among the "primary" Boom writers, could also boast of living exclusively off the earnings from his writing).

Puig is, moreover, an extremely important writer in relation to the direction of the contemporary Latin American novel. Until he burst belatedly onto the literary scene with *La traición de Rita Hayworth* (*Betrayed by Rita Hayworth*) in 1968, bringing to his fiction a profound understanding of popular culture and viewing it not Olympically but up-close and sympathetically, the "new" novel was working its way through two chief options: the neobaroque (Carlos Fuentes's *The Death of Artemio Cruz* [1962] and José Lezama Lima's *Paradiso* [1966] would be two strong examples) and the self-conscious encyclopedia (such as Cortázar's *Hopscotch* [1963], Vargas Llosa's *The Green House* [1966], and García Márquez's *One Hundred Years of Solitude* [1967]). But neither the neobaroque novel nor the self-conscious encyclopedic novel breaks through the barrier of literary modernism's tendency to treat Culture reverently, as something sacred and apart from the degraded commodities of everyday life. In breaking through to a postmodern, culturally unpretentious space ("modern" and "postmodern" will be explained more fully in due time), Puig made an impact that was so immense that soon such leaders as Cortázar, Vargas Llosa, and Donoso were producing fictions based on movie stars (*Queremos tanto a Glenda* [*We Love Glenda So Much*]), melodramatic soap operas (*La tía Julia y el escribidor* [*Aunt Julia and the Scriptwriter*]), detective novels (*¿Quién mató a Palomino Molero?* [*Who Killed Palomino Molero?*]), and erotic mysteries (*La misteriosa desaparición de la Marquesita de Loria* [The mysterious disappearance of the Marchioness of Loria]).

This volume on Manuel Puig has both a set of underlying assumptions and a unifying purpose. The principal assumptions maintain that Puig's work is both unique and substantial, and therefore ought to be explored systematically, in a way scholars have yet to do. The purpose, consequently, is to explore Manuel Puig's variegated oeuvre and to observe how certain constant concerns (among which figure prominently the roles the unconscious and the mass media play in individual and societal behavior, the irrepressible urge for erotic satisfaction, the value of orality, the need for humor, the pain of estrangement and self-estrangement, the power of cliché, the spell of spectacle, and the complexity of the commonplace) recombine and play off one another, and off more ephemeral motifs as well. A secondary purpose would be to give Puig's later works (his novels after *Kiss of the Spider Woman* as well as his nonnarrative texts) a more sustained and methodical treatment than they have to date been afforded. I do not share the widespread opinion that Puig went into a tailspin during what turned out to be the last decade of his life. "Tropics of Decline," the chapter devoted to his last two novels, is where I argue most emphatically to the contrary.

My research methods are probably best described as eclectic. I have availed myself of every journalistic book review, every interview, scholarly article, and published book on Puig I could obtain. Occasionally I take recourse to literary theory, especially the insights into narrative discourse of Mikhail Bakhtin (Puig's soulmate in pluralism), and to the psychoanalytic theories of Freud, which profoundly shaped Puig's worldview even as he criticized them and narrowed their scope. More than anything, however, I have relied on close readings of the primary sources (in both Spanish and English), feedback from my students at Cornell, and personal contact with the author, whose fascination for and identification with Western popular culture – in both the Hollywood and Occidental senses – I unembarrassedly share. Accordingly, I avoid using technical terms wherever possible and hasten to explain their sense in common parlance where such use is unavoidable. After considering numerous potential ways of organizing my material (Puig's works have been studied according to their geographic setting or place of composition; their allusion to popular cultural genres; their formal attributes such as dialogue, stream of consciousness, omniscient narration, and the like), I have opted for a straightforward, chronological presentation. Such an ordering, though pedestrian in appearance, even while it constitutes a not uncritical allusion to generic constraints, still reflects the approximate process through which the author's imagination developed.

Acknowledgments

This book owes its existence, first and foremost, to Manuel Puig, whose shining presence, even at its most somber, I miss palpably. The interview with which we planned to conclude this study unfortunately never took place. I also owe a great debt of gratitude to series editor David William Foster, whose patience I tried on many an occasion. His suggestions for revision were invariably constructive and helpful. I wish to thank as well Gonzalo Díaz Migoyo, who generously shared with me years of research into Puig's early work. Thanks, too, to Djelal Kadir for granting permission to reproduce substantial portions of a chronology compiled by David D. Clark for the Autumn 1991 issue of *World Literature Today*. Copyright ©1991 by the University of Oklahoma Press. In the computer age, one no longer has a typist to thank. But one fortunately still has a family, and mine, composed of my parents, Florence and Herbert Tittler, my children, Mara and Ethan Tittler, and my wife, Susan Hill, provides the sort of unflagging support that mere thanks could never repay. It is to them, and to all Manuel Puig's present and future readers, that I dedicate this volume.

Chronology

1932	Manuel Puig Delledonne born 28 December in General Villegas (Buenos Aires Province), Argentina.
1936	Develops a love for moviegoing, accompanying his mother to see films.
1942	Begins to study English.
1946	Completes elementary school. Moves to Buenos Aires to attend boarding school.
1950	Enters the school of architecture at the University of Buenos Aires.
1956	Travels to Rome with a scholarship to study at the Centro Sperimentale di Cinematografia.
1958	Moves to London, where he gives lessons in Spanish and Italian and works as a dishwasher.
1960	Returns to Argentina. Works as an assistant director of Argentine films.
1961-1962	Back in Rome, working on films, when working.
1963	Moves to New York. Works for Air France at Idlewild (now JFK) Airport and begins writing his first novel.
1965	Finishes novel *La tración de Rita Hayworth*. Visits Tahiti. In December *La traición* is a finalist for the Seix Barral publishing house's Biblioteca Breve Prize; Puig signs a contract, but the novel runs into censorship problems.
1968	After further censorship problems in Argentina, the novel is finally published in Buenos Aires by a small firm called Editorial Jorge Alvarez.
1969	Gallimard publishes French translation of *La traición*, and in June the work is selected by *Le Monde* as one

of the best novels of 1968-69. In September Puig's second novel, *Boquitas pintadas*, is published and becomes a best-seller.

1971   First English translation of Puig's work, *Betrayed by Rita Hayworth*, is published in New York.

1973   His third novel, *The Buenos Aires Affair*, appears. *Heartbreak Tango* (the English translation of *Boquitas pintadas*) is published in New York.

1974   *Boquitas pintadas*, adapted for the screen by Puig for Argentine director Leopoldo Torre Nilsson, is awarded the best-script prize at the San Sebastián Film Festival.

1976   Puig returns to New York after spending about two years in Mexico. His fourth novel, *El beso de la mujer araña* (Kiss of the spider woman) appears. The English version of *The Buenos Aires Affair* is published in New York.

1978   Puig's film adaptation of José Donoso's *El lugar sin límites* garners the best-script prize at San Sebastián.

1979   His fifth novel, *Pubis angelical*, and *Kiss of the Spider Woman* are published.

1980   His sixth novel, *Maldición eterna a quien lea estas páginas* (Eternal curse on the reader of these pages) appears.

1981   Puig moves to Rio de Janeiro.

1982   His seventh novel, *Sangre de amor correspondido* (Blood of requited love), and *Eternal Curse on the Reader of These Pages* are published.

1983   Puig publishes a two-act play, *Bajo un manto de estrellas*, in Barcelona.

1984   *Blood of Requited Love* appears in New York.

1985   English version of Puig's play *Bajo un manto de estrellas* (*Under a Mantle of Stars*) is published in New York. Film version of *Kiss of the Spider Woman*, directed by Héctor Babenco, is released.

1986   English version of *Pubis Angelical* and of the play *Kiss of the Spider Woman* are published.

1987   *Kiss of the Spider Woman: The Screenplay* is published in Boston.

1988   His eighth novel, *Cae la noche tropical* (Tropical night falling) appears. The English version of the play *El misterio del ramo de rosas* (*Mystery of the Rose Bouquet*) is published in London.

1989   Puig moves to Cuernavaca, Mexico, with his mother.

1990   Dies on 22 July in Cuernavaca, suffering cardiac arrest following routine gall bladder surgery. His remains are buried in General Villegas, Argentina.

1991   English edition of *Tropical Night Falling* is published in New York.

Chapter One

Coming Attractions

The name of Manuel Puig has for almost 25 years brought with it associations with popular or mass culture. He is, to be sure, not the first Latin American author to have paid attention to the underclasses that make up the bulk of the society around him. The numerous works of the Caribbean slave narrative of the nineteenth century[1] and of the Mexican Revolution in the early years of the twentieth[2] (to name just two major subgenres of the Spanish-American novel) readily attest to the long-standing tradition of social commitment in Latin American letters. But Puig's method of dealing with the subject matter was indeed novel. His enduring innovation, we can safely say now, resides in his incorporating the cultural by-products of certain midcentury technological advancements that, for better or worse, have served to link less developed regions (often termed the Third World) with the metropolitan centers of Western civilization. The diverse effects of these largely commercially inspired, cliché-ridden, and sentimentally oriented mass-entertainment products on often impressionable psyches constitute a hallmark of Puig's creativity.

But the mere fact of representing such a charged scenario only begins to explain the ultimate significance of Puig's achievement. Other than being recognized as the first writer to venture boldly into this risky terrain, it is the manner in which Puig exposes the alienating neocolonial circumstance that sets him apart. The concrete narrative techniques employed have proven to vary largely from work to work – and some works, like his second novel, *Boquitas pintadas* (*Heartbreak Tango*, 1969) and the more recent *Sangre de amor correspondido* (*Blood of Requited Love*, 1982), are strikingly original in the devices they employ and their effects. But one feature has remained constant throughout the eight novels that run from *La traición de Rita Hayworth* (*Betrayed by Rita Hayworth*, 1968) to *Cae la noche tropical* (*Tropical Night Falling*, 1988): narrative omniscience is systematically excluded from the author's ample repertoire.[3] Narratives representing the psychological impact of cultural expansion, conveyed via a tenaciously held discursive pluralism, constitute the unique textuality of Manuel Puig's oeuvre.

What replaces the authoritative discourse of the traditional omniscient narrator is an array of voices, arranged in no definite hierarchy, that enter into a complex, shifting dynamic. Occasionally the dialogue is overt and unified, as when in the first chapter of *Betrayed by Rita Hayworth* Mita's family chats casually at home about nothing in particular (see chapter 2 of this volume). Dialogue in this conventional sense (to the exclusion of virtually all other discursive models) forms the basis of three of Puig's later novels, *El beso de la mujer araña* (*Kiss of the Spider Woman*, 1976), *Maldición eterna a quien lea estas Páginas* (*Eternal Curse on the Reader of These Pages*, 1980), and the aforementioned *Tropical Night Falling*. More often, however, the interplay of voices occurs in the reader's mind, as when the discourse of one chapter is juxtaposed with that of another, when writing appears alongside spoken language, or when a specific character or work is compared intertextually with an established type or entire literary genre. The result of such verbal montages is a strangely decentered, open, polyphonic (multitonal) sort of novel in which the relativity of truth is set in high relief against the absolutism of society's dominant power structures.

The obviously subversive notion of dialogism (etymologically, "two wordism"), formulated mainly during the 1920s and 1930s by the Soviet theorist Mikhail Bakhtin, provides much of the conceptual framework for this study on the novels of Manuel Puig.[4] Although reading with an eye toward dialogism does not illuminate everything of potential significance in Puig's fiction (no single method may honestly make that claim), it does open some important areas of inquiry. Whereas one may be tempted to dismiss the absence of a narrating authority figure as a mere stylistic tic, the dialogic model ensures disclosure of the crucial link between Puig's technique and his subtly tendentious thematics. Dialogism penetrates the surface of particular utterances to reveal them as what Bakhtin calls "language images," representing the idioms of particular social strata.[5]

Since the linguistic portrayal of social tensions is virtually ubiquitous in Puig's fiction, tracing its trajectory and ramifications inevitably entails confronting the implied author's underlying ideology. That is, if we consider a text's configuration to be the statement of a particular authorial voice, then the way that statement interacts with the themes also being evoked cannot help but resonate in the work's overall effect and significance. The seemingly neutral formal feature of narrative perspectivism in Puig's fiction leads to such pertinent contemporary issues as the stability of personal identity, the accessibility of historical truth, the nature of sexuality, the morality of exercising power, the banalization of art, and the role of criticism. Treating the works of Manuel Puig dialogically helps explain why, of all the brilliant Spanish-American writers to have emerged in the past 30 years, only Puig rivals García Márquez in terms of recognition by an audience so broad as to encompass a multitude of general readers and professional critics alike.

In keeping with the heightened awareness Bakhtin imparts of the forces at play in narrative discourse, the following biographical sketch should be understood as a partial (both incomplete and biased) narrative account of Puig's life and works. The life and works themselves are viewed as narratives, not because they exist wholly within language but because it is only through language that we can gain (again, partial) access to objects and events. This is therefore a text about other texts, even as it seeks to reflect the world beyond symbols and signs. As one of Puig's characters in *Under a Mantle of Stars* says of some old friends who died almost 20 years previous, "We can't possibly remember them as they were."[6] Because of both the vagaries of memory and language's tendency to refer to other signs rather than directly to the raw components of the world, extralinguistic reality remains forever beyond our grasp. The most we can aspire to is a more-or-less faithful symbolic reconstruction, to which future versions in turn may consciously or inadvertently refer.

Manuel Puig Delledonne was born on 28 December 1932 in General Villegas (Buenos Aires Province), Argentina, a small town lost in that country's endless pampas. Puig's provincial environment had little to offer a sensitive, effeminate child. Fortunately for Manuel his mother took him daily from the age of four to the local moviehouse, where he could partake of a world of Hollywood glamour, fulfillment, and heartbreak. His favorite stars were Ginger Rogers and Eleanor Powell for musicals and Marlene Dietrich and Greta Garbo for drama. Such was his infatuation with American films that at the age of 10 he undertook the study of English, a language he already knew in good measure from growing up at the movies.

At 13 Puig finished his primary education and was sent to boarding school in Buenos Aires. To his disconcertion, he discovered that life there differed little from that in General Villegas: one prosaic day followed another, with not a shadow of the sublimity or romance he sought. Although Puig claims to have read little, there is evidence that during these years he became familiar with Gide, Hesse, Huxley, and Sartre, among other writers. After graduating from high school, he continued to float somewhat aimlessly, enrolling in the University of Buenos Aires first in philosophy and then in architecture, neither of which careers he pursued to completion. While at the university, however, he did manage to study more English, as well as French and Italian (the "languages of film").

When in 1955 Puig won a scholarship to study at the Centro Sperimentale di Cinematografia in Italy, it appeared he had finally found a way out of the monotony and machismo of his parochial surroundings. But his inability to assert his authority eventually (after returning to Argentina in 1960 and going back to Italy a second time in 1961) convinced him that producing films was not his forte. In 1963, with no career as yet defined and several failed attempts at writing film scripts in English, he moved to New York, took a job with Air France, and began to write in Spanish a series of interior monologues based upon many of the events and characters of his childhood. By 1965 that text had grown into the novel *Betrayed by Rita Hayworth*.

In December of that year the novel was chosen as a finalist in the Seix Barral publishing house's Biblioteca Breve Prize and was slated for expeditious publication. When censorship problems (it is not clear whether they are attributable to the Franco dictatorship or to internal matters at the Barcelona publishing house) led to repeated delays, he decided to try to find an editor in Argentina. The novel's controversial content again led to censorship problems, and it was not until 1968, with the Latin American novelistic "Boom" in full swing, when Editorial Jorge Alvarez, a small firm in Buenos Aires, finally published the book. Puig's first measure of international success came when the novel's French translation was published by the prestigious Parisian publisher Gallimard. In June 1969 the leading daily newspaper *Le Monde* selected *Rita Hayworth* as one of the 10 best novels of 1968-69. On top of that triumph came the September 1969 publication of Puig's second novel, *Boquitas pintadas (Heartbreak Tango)*, based largely on the author's experiences upon returning home after his visit to Italy. An immediate best-seller, *Heartbreak Tango* turned Puig into as much of a celebrity in his own country as he already was in France.

In the 1970s, when for reasons political, personal, and literary the novelistic Boom showed signs of sputtering, Puig's career soared. His first two novels appeared in English translation in 1971 and 1973, respectively (rather than assigning the task to a translator, Puig worked very closely in reelaborating these and other texts). In 1973 he completed his third novel, *The Buenos Aires Affair: A Detective Novel*, confirming his reputation as a prolific and original writer of popular and popularizing fiction. Puig's versatility became apparent when in 1974 his screen adaptation of *Boquitas pintadas* won the best-script prize at Spain's San Sebastián Film Festival. After living in Mexico for about two years (late 1973-76), Puig moved back to New York, where he wrote, largely in protest of Argentina's military government's *guerra sucia* (dirty war) against dissidents, *El beso de la mujer araña (Kiss of the Spider Woman* [1976]), widely considered his greatest work. The novel was published in Barcelona by Seix Barral, the same publisher that would not or could not publish his first novel and the publisher of all his later novels in Spanish. That same year saw the publication of *The Buenos Aires Affair* in English. Two years later he adapted another novel, José Donoso's *El lugar sin límites (Hell Has No Limits)*, for the screen, and again he won the best-script prize at San Sebastián. Following the pattern of previous novels, in 1979 the English version of *Spider Woman* appeared, along with the original version of Puig's fifth novel, *Pubis angelical*. *Maldición eterna a quien lea estas páginas (Eternal Curse on the Reader of These Pages)*, set in New York and written originally in English, reached the public in 1980.

In the 1980s Puig maintained the impressive rhythm of productivity of the previous decade. As he explored more tragic plotlines, gave less emphasis to popular cultural forms, and moved into non-narrative creative spaces, however, he accordingly received less critical attention. To get away from the "open sewer" New York had become and to be closer to his aging parents, he moved in 1981 to Rio de Janeiro. The following year he published his seventh novel,

Sangre de amor correspondido (*Blood of Requited Love*), which he
wrote in Portuguese. *Eternal Curse* appeared in English that year as
well. In 1983 he published a volume of dramatic texts containing the
plays *Bajo un mantel de estrellas* (*Under a Mantle of Stars*) and the
stage adaptation of his novel *Kiss of the Spider Woman*. That same
year also saw the publication of Puig's short stories in a San Francisco anthology of gay Latin American fiction, *My Deep Dark Pain Is
Love*. English translations of his recent works continued to appear
regularly: *Blood of Requited Love* in New York in 1984 and *Under a
Mantle of Stars* in 1985. That year also marked the release of the
enormously successful film version of *Kiss of the Spider Woman*,
directed by the Brazilian Héctor Babenco and starring William Hurt,
Raúl Juliá, and Sonia Braga. Hurt later won an Academy Award and
the best-actor award at Cannes for his performance as Molina. If Puig
were one of his own fictional characters, he could be described at
this point as having fulfilled his fated encounter with the silver
screen or having completed a trajectory begun when he was four
years old.

In 1986, the dramatic version of *The Kiss of the Spider Woman*
appeared (note the definite article in its title, which Puig did not use
in the novel and filmscript), as did (belatedly) the English translation
of *Pubis Angelical*. The next year Puig was awarded an honorary
doctorate from the University of Aberdeen and *Kiss of the Spider
Woman: The Screenplay* was published in Boston. In 1988, after a
six-year novelistic hiatus, he published his eighth novel, *Cae la
noche tropical* (*Tropical Night Falling*), and in London the English
translation of his third play, *El misterio del ramo de rosas* (*Mystery
of the Rose Bouquet*), appeared. Both marked the author's return to
a more lighthearted vein of writing. The following year he moved
with his mother, María Luisa Delledonne de Puig, to Cuernavaca,
Mexico. Only months later, on 22 July 1990, Puig died there of complications following a routine gall bladder operation. In 1991 the
English translation of *Tropical Night Falling* was published in New
York. Two short stories, "The Usual Suspects" and "Relative Humidity 95%," also appeared, as did in his honor two special issues of
academic journals, *Review of Contemporary Fiction* and *World Literature Today*. The issue of the latter journal, titled *The Posthumous
Career of Manuel Puig*, appears to bolster the contention that this
account ought to be continued.

Chapter Two

Where Is Father?

Betrayed by Rita Hayworth

Whatever else may be said about Manuel Puig's first work, *Betrayed by Rita Hayworth* (1968) stands as a daringly experimental novel.[1] It is an attempt to create a convincing, valid fictional world without taking recourse to conventionally hierarchized narrative techniques. Narrative authority, traditionally concentrated in an omniscient author figure, is here diffused among numerous narrating characters, none of whom can claim impartiality or privilege as concerns the "truth." Instead of a powerful paternal monologue, the reader encounters a complex network of voices rarely heard in literature: the young, the poor, the ill, the female, the sexually ambivalent. Given the profusion of fragmentary perspectives, one might expect the text to fall into cacophony and confusion. During the 20-odd years since its initial appearance, however, the novel, which after getting past the censors in Spain and Argentina enjoyed a favorable popular reception, has steadily grown in critical stature. The reason? The extraordinarily well-achieved integration of its dominant thematic strand with the manner in which that motif is conveyed. The absence of a paternal authority figure, which proves to be the key to understanding the main character's motivation, doubles as the guiding principle for the text's composition.

"When the cat's away, the mice will play." This trite old maxim represents on more than one level the system that underlies the novelistic discourse in *Betrayed by Rita Hayworth*. On the most obvious level, a single, relatively concise and authoritative narrator (the cat) yields his place to numerous small and garrulous figures (the mice). But let us not forget we are dealing with a proverb, the very embodiment of cliché language. On a second, performative plane, therefore, we may find that the mice's chatter tends not so much toward the solemn or sublime as toward the hackneyed or banal.

These narrator-proxies' idea of culture, for instance, might be a soccer game, a maudlin bolero, or at best a Fred Astaire and Ginger Rogers movie. Although the last might seem exotic to a landlocked Argentinean of the 1930s and 1940s, none of the three would qualify as thought-provoking or spiritually uplifting fare. But there is more. As the character-narrators exchange impressions of everyday life, the novel too enters into a fruitful dialogue with its literary genre, The Novel. Much as Cervantes does in *Don Quixote*, Puig asks questions as to the proper sorts of matter for novelistic discourse – the place of heroism, suspense, humor, and the like. And he raises those issues of decorum not in an entirely neutral manner but through a narrative form that already deviates from the norm. The work thus assumes a posture inherently at odds with the typical on both fronts: that of serious high culture as well as that of the less nuanced mass culture. Neither complacently aristocratic nor formulaically commercial, *Betrayed by Rita Hayworth* (and, it turns out, Puig's fiction in general) carves out an innovative middle ground that combines cherished egalitarian values with acute artistic self-consciousness.

To appreciate fully how this novel establishes the basis for all the others, let us follow its initial development one chapter at a time. Although somewhat plain, this approach yields results whose substance more than compensates for any lack in flair or flash.

The novel's assault on autocracy begins not with the first word of the first chapter, but before: with the title. Here the author places before the reader his interpretation of the novel's substance, an utterance that eventually must be reconciled with the text it precedes. Rather than jump prematurely into an explanation of the title's significance, however, I merely note for future reference the evocation of one of the silver screen's all-time glamour queens, in curious association with the insidious notion of betrayal. The sinister play of reality and appearances, as well as the paramount role of film in certain characters' lives and in the life of the novel, will become clear soon enough. What matters for now is to observe the very visible presence of an author figure, despite the absence of a conventionally authorial narrator.[2] That same, seemingly helpful author figure is responsible for the heading just below the chapter number, which reads "Mita's Parents' Place, La Plata, 1933" (7). Analogous information (the place, the date, and, if applicable, the speaker) is provided at the start of each of the 16 chapters.

Within the chapter itself, however, the reader finds surprisingly little in the way of orienting markers. The discourse emerges as a series of disembodied voices, devoid of any explicit action. Identifying the speakers and following the thread of the conversations amount to quite a challenge, and meeting that challenge turns out to be the reader's main role, here and elsewhere, in the dialogue with the text. It is soon apparent that, although the characters are in dialogue with one another, they are not always in communication. Some themes repeat themselves obsessively, while others, thanks to well-placed non sequiturs, ramble off into oblivion. Within the everyday family setting, individuals are not differentiated as to age or sex. Ideas, too, undergo an essential blending and leveling, such that matters relating to cooking, shopping, and medicine run into and carry the same weight as those of morality, sentiment, and entertainment. The colloquial and familiar language used throughout represents faithfully the cadences and verbal peculiarities of the spoken idiom. Yet such unpretentious domesticity coexists oddly with the unfamiliarity of its presentation as Literature.

The ultimate effect of this slice of small-town pampas life, whose primary function is to set the novel's scene and tone, is negative. Not much happens. Nothing of import is resolved in the end (this may be said of the entire novel as well). Meaning in the normal sense of the term does not emerge. No character stands out from the others, except perhaps Mita, the daughter who has married and moved away. The family misses her and worries about her and her infant son, Toto. If anything, it is her *absence* that gives dimension to her identity. Mita's absence, of course, reflects and reinforces that of the missing narrator, establishing absence as a formal precept within the text. Rare privilege thus gravitates to the dialogue as an element in the novelistic discourse.

Chapter 2 ("At Berto's, Vallejos, 1933") repeats many of the motifs found in chapter 1, with some significant additions. As before, dialogue replaces narration as the chosen mode of presentation. The roles of the author figure and reader (in what we may call unfamiliar intimacy) thus remain essentially unchanged. Action, other than language in motion, is reduced to a milk delivery (19-20) and the writing of a letter by Mita's husband, Berto, in the adjacent room (another form of language in motion). The discourse is again a rambling, imprecise, and repetitive conversation, with Mita once more elsewhere. The infant Toto is present, but only as an uncomprehending interlocutor ("But you shitty little bedbug, you don't even know how to talk yet" [23]). And for all we know (although it need not be so), the chitchat in this chapter may be squarely contemporaneous with that of the one just encountered. Mita may have left her old home behind. But judging from the form of chapter 2, the petty pace of daily existence goes on in much the same way in her new one.

Here, though, it is two servants, Felisa and Amparo, who speak. Their language is more proletarian than that of Mita's family, sprinkled as it is with obscenity, fears of bearing illegitimate children for exploitative masters, and descriptions of undisguised poverty. Despite some obvious financial problems (the milk is bought on credit), the presence of servants indicates the family belongs solidly to the Argentinean middle class. The almost absolute power that the ill-tempered Berto wields over the servant girls, moreover, comes across forcefully. Domestic intrigue enters, too, as insinuations arise to the effect that Berto and Amparo share a secret to which Mita is not privy. But even though Berto is generally acknowledged as good looking (he is compared here and in chapter 1 to the movie star Carlos Palau), he is not a womanizer. The patient reader has to wait until the very last chapter to ascertain that their deceit is relatively innocent, having to do with Berto's resentment over Mita's failure to defend him in a discussion she had with her sister. That concluding chapter discloses the full text of Berto's letter, as well as finally baring his frustrated male soul. The primary function of this chapter, in addition to restating and developing the principle of absence (no conventional action, no maternal figure, a distant authoritarian father, no paternal narrator), is to lay the groundwork for that future dialogue.

Chapter 3, "Toto, 1939," introduces a mode of writing and a character that eventually come to dominate the novel. The narrator-character is a six-year-old child who thinks or talks to himself at home. The mode of writing is, of course, narration in the first-person singular and, more specifically, interior monologue. But this monologue is at bottom a dialogue, as the child's first sentence, directed toward "Mommy," indicates. At first actual and later imaginary, the conversations go beyond evoking an ideal listener. By incorporating embedded quotations of various other characters important to Toto (Felisa, Pocha Pérez, Berto, and chiefly Mita), the child's thought processes are shown to function according to a dialogic principle. His point of view, if we may call it that, consists of an amalgamation of diverse points of view: some contradictory, some coincidental, some simply different. In keeping with the narrator's youth, the normally distinct realms of fantasy, memory, description, and speech separate and merge, often without transition. These various idioms coexist simultaneously in the character's developing psyche.

Amidst the superficial disorder of Toto's narration, certain motifs do stand out. One is the child's fascination with films, several of which (*Romeo and Juliet*, *The Great Ziegfeld*, *Snow White*, and an unnamed Shirley Temple film) he recounts in detail.[3] Another is the patent sexual content of some of the passages. That Toto confuses some aspects of his life with situations he has seen in the movies and that he misunderstands a good deal of what he sees, especially the parts with sexual connotations, are basic to this section. But despite (or perhaps because of) Toto's relative unawareness, film and sex are shown to collude and play a major role in the evolution of his personal identity. For what is conveyed amounts to a classic Oedipal drama, replete with its primal scene, attempted parricide, and eventual castration of the son by the father.[4] The primal scene is predictably absent from view. It takes place "offstage" between the couple that celebrate their conjugal rites during the daily siesta hour. Excluded from the scene, Toto spends the hour thinking about the films he sees with his mother. Those daydreams represent the viewings during which he symbolically attempts to usurp his father's position in the relationship. According to Toto's memory, Berto has already responded to the threat by having the boy taken to the girl's bathroom at the charity show. This humiliation undercuts the son's masculinity, leading him to prefer film to reality and his mother's petticoats to his father's pants ("I hide my head between Daddy's pants legs! but much better for hiding are your petticoats because I can hide my head and if Daddy opens your legs they see me").[5] The Freudian conflict, so disordered in its telling, has pronounced resonance and far-reaching psychological consequences later in the novel. Imparted sympathetically from the perspective of the powerless child, the chapter begins to explain the insurrection against narrative authority so prevalent already in the text.

A less fundamental but still important aspect of chapter 3 is its introduction of a series of references for later development. One allusion is to Héctor, Toto's cousin, who narrates his own chapter in the novel's second part ("Héctor isn't my brother, Mommy says Héctor is my cousin but his mother is sick and Héctor lives in my house but he doesn't play with me and the picture cards" [30]). Another is to Choli, who figures prominently in what Lucille Kerr, following Bakhtin, has called the "hidden dialogue" of chapter 5 (Kerr, 57) ("Choli couldn't take it [the pigeon] on the train, she went away forever to Buenos Aires 'The only friend I have in Vallejos' and she went away" [29]). And a third prefiguration resides in the young Toto's reference to himself at a later stage of his life. These lines – "once I woke Mommy up during naptime because I'm bored and Daddy 'I never slapped you but the day I put my hands on you I'll break you in two' and I'm going to think about the movie I like the best" (28) – express a symptomatic evasion of traumatic memories and a drift toward a world of fantasy. Rather than an ever-worsening neurosis, though, that defensive move proves to be nothing more than an intermediate step in the process of artistic creation.

Before plunging definitively into the minds of the character-narrators, the novel provides in chapter 4 ("Choli's Conversation with Mita, 1941") one more example of a dialogue in the conventional sense of the term. But the form this dialogue takes hardly qualifies as standard, for the words of only one of the participants, those of Choli, appear on the printed page. The responses of her consistently absent interlocutor, represented by a dash and a blank space, must be inferred from Choli's continued prattling. One of the triumphs of *Betrayed by Rita Hayworth* lies in the fact that this "hidden dialogue" manages to inform the reader sufficiently. This owes largely to the way in which Choli is conceived, as someone with virtually no depth to her, such that her utterances elicit responses in a highly predictable pattern. More a caricature than a portrait, Choli's characterization complicates and intensifies the motif of deception, incorporating the added dimension of self-deceit. The novel's last manifestation of surface phenomena (what the characters say rather than what they think and feel), this chapter marks a temporary swerve in the text's trajectory toward an emphatic sociological critique.

Why come down so hard on Choli? Simply because she incorporates uncritically many of the most insidious qualities of commercialized, mass-mediated contemporary existence. An itinerant salesperson for Hollywood Cosmetics, Choli has swallowed the company's sales pitch whole. Her head is full of notions about being "interesting," impressing men with small talk, flashy clothes, and foundation makeup. When on the road, she spends her free time in her hotel room trying on clothes and admiring herself in the mirror. And she is so blind to her trivial vanity that she has no shame in confessing, "it's so much fun, a pity I can't take pictures of myself" (52). Her ignorance, which includes believing that London is the chic part of the United States and that individuals fall easily into neat categories ("I'm the American woman type" [40]), extends to her own self-entrapment. Convinced she is a liberated woman ("No, Mita, my troubles are over, luckily it's different now at Hollywood Cosmetics, with the freedom I have" [46]), she is resolutely unaware of the way in which her adopted identity as a femme fatale reduces her to an object of men's sexual fantasies.

To be sure, Choli is not wholly antipathetic. She has lost her husband, first – when he was alive – to other women and later to death. She is both a dedicated mother and a breadwinner for her son. And she is, on the whole, a supportive and amenable companion where Mita is concerned. But these ameliorating characteristics are undercut by two craftily employed techniques. First, their context: they are buried in the middle of the chapter, where they receive only minor emphasis. And second, the means by which they are conveyed: Choli's entire attempt at communicating (one might even say "communing") with Mita is carried out via the telephone. This remarkable contrivance, which is purported to eliminate the distance between speakers, cannot ultimately allow us to "reach out and touch someone." What does Mita know, after all, of Choli's gestures during their chat? Could Choli not, as she extols the virtues of pancake and blush, be playing Narcissus before her looking glass? Admittedly better than not getting in touch at all, Choli's technologically mediated contact is assuredly no match, where deep mutual understanding is concerned, for a face-to-face encounter.

In one of the first serious approaches to this novel, the Uruguayan critic Emir Rodríguez Monegal stated that *Betrayed by Rita Hayworth* is concerned at bottom with the alienation of language.[6] By that he meant that the characters employ a stale, ill-fitting speech, borrowed from the world of film, advertisements, and other foreign and idealized realms. When they try to apply that imposed medium to their lives the results are predictably disastrous, for unrealistic expectations inevitably lead to crushing defeats. Although Rodríguez Monegal's claims are not uniformly valid throughout the novel (Toto, among others, eventually demonstrates a creative and incipiently critical use of language), the chapter dedicated to Choli is without a doubt a fine example of alienated language. But only when Choli's voice enters into dialogue with Mita's sober and tragic discourse (chapter 8) can we appreciate the full force of her pathetic mistaking of glamour for beauty.

In chapter 5 ("Toto, 1942") the novel's focus returns for the first time to a character-narrator already somewhat developed. This is the first strong indication that Toto will be the work's protagonist, although in many respects (his youth, his lack of heroism or other exemplary qualities, the modest proportion of the novel he occupies) he fails to meet the usual criteria. Nonetheless, since no other character plays a role nearly so major in the fiction, we can say he is at least relatively protagonistic.

The re-presentation of Toto invites comparison and contrast with his first appearance in the novel. In the three years since his last monologue, as one might expect, Toto has not entirely abandoned his childish ways. His incomprehension where matters sexual are concerned is such that some critics have alleged it already demonstrates a problematic repression, an unhealthy mental block. Furthermore, as the first part of the chapter again takes place during the siesta hour (when he must "kill" time, if not his father), it is not surprising that his relationship with his parents remains largely unchanged. This is especially evident in Berto's trying to make a "man" of him ("men don't cry" [62]) as well as in Toto's attempt to convince Berto to join him and Mita at the movies. Although Toto is no longer so concerned about "the gypsy" (a bogeyman figure in his earlier monologue), his tendency to see things in terms of good and bad, as well as an excessive attention to his rank in class and other considerations of questionable significance, mark this narrator as an extension of the little boy previously seen.

He does, however, display signs of growth. For one thing, he observes that Lalo is poor and Indian (54; *negro* in the original, 75) and that Alicita's aunt's husband works in the same bank where the servant Felisa's mother waxes the floors (58), showing an awareness of some of the differences between the social classes with which he has contact. For another, his esthetic sense, which was precociously advanced at age six, appears to be even more refined now, as his detailed description of Alicita's tresses reveals (56). But it is his awareness of the conflictive nature of human interaction, reflected in his description of Rita Hayworth, the leading actress in *Blood and Sand,* as treacherous ("she's always betraying somebody" [63]) that undergoes the greatest evolution. Rita's betrayal and treachery certainly do not refer just to her leading man, Tyrone Power. As mentioned, Toto was counting on her seducing his father into sharing with him and Mita the star-studded world of film. Instead, she induces in Toto a hope of plenitude – of family harmony forever after – that goes unfulfilled. (More on the title's many possible meanings still later).

As if the lesson of the film were not sufficiently clear, life steps in to reinforce it. In the second part of the chapter (like the text as a whole, the chapter consists of two parts of unequal length), Toto suffers an amorous disillusion when Alicita abandons him in favor of his rival, Luisito Castro. Toto's status as a mere spectator of heterosexual relations appears to be determined when he later happens upon the adolescents Paquita and Raúl García involved in some heavy petting. In view of its extremely diffuse shape, one need not consider the story of Toto's childhood "a classic study of the development of homosexuality," as Norman Lavers has phrased it.[7] But in this chapter at least, Toto's trajectory, which runs from aspiring suitor to dejected voyeur, apparently marks him for a life on the margins of society.

As chapters 6 and 7 ("Teté, Winter, 1942" and "Delia, Summer, 1943") deal with narrating characters who are in many ways analogous, it is reasonable to group these chapters together. Both have minor young female characters, with little transcendence for the rest of the novel. While their presence adds some dimension and detail to the fictional world, their chief function is to provide illuminating comparative perspectives on the intensifying relations among the members of Toto's family.

Teté, already identified by Toto as a "rich kid" ("*ricachona*" [97] in the original; "luscious" [70] is correct but misses the point of her social class), comes from a family of landowners. Delia, on the other hand, reveals herself as a social-climbing servant who aspires to the level of wealth she sees about her in Mita and Berto's house.

Having been jilted by her true love, López, Delia is determined to rise out of her servitude by marrying Yamil, a plain-looking Turkish man with a strong work ethic. Mita helps her in this undertaking, and this generosity in assisting Delia is consistent with her offering to care for Teté while Mita's sister (Teté's mother) is ill. This nurturing quality is further corroborated by her accepting Teté as a member of the household while another, disruptive member of the extended family, Héctor, has already been granted an extended stay.

As befits their different stations in life, Teté and Delia do not share the same diction. The 12-year-old Teté still tends toward the use of puerile expressions, depending frequently on onomatopoeia ("Did you see the little parrots pic-pac against the wall, it's because they don't see, like they're blind" [83]). Delia, at 21, is (with Héctor and Cobito) one of the novel's most verbally expressive character-narrators. Her use of diminutives, augmentatives, summary judgments, and colorful figures of speech (as in "that bitch playing the little girl with the lace collar and all, the old cow. No waist whatsoever and stumps for legs" [91]) lends wit and variety to the thematically grim reflection on provincial life.

Individual styles aside, however, both narrators concur in portraying Toto's problematic maturation process. Still fascinated with the magical world of film, according to Teté, Toto fails to learn how to ride a bicycle, much to Berto's disappointment. When the father punishes Toto by removing his moviegoing privileges, the boy shows signs of suffering a veritable trauma. In a later episode related by Delia, Toto reacts to Héctor's taunts about his inability to learn how to swim by stabbing a servant with a fork. Although the scene is a fictional level removed from the reader (Delia remembers it while she does her evening chores), the degree of action embodied and the suspense created in its recounting (through the use of the refrain "what happened the day before yesterday didn't surprise me" [95 and passim]) mark Delia's account as one of the most readerly in the series. This impression is in no way diminished by the consideration that Delia's receptiveness to Héctor's linguistic incursions (she reproduces his slang-ridden line, "Iron the pipes of my new threads good so I won't go out looking like a yokel" [94]; "*planchame bien los talompas de la pilcha nueva, no me las hagas ir de gilastro*" [131] in the original) later takes on an unmistakably sexual aspect.

In chapter 8 ("Mita, Winter, 1943"), after a long process of preparation, the novel finally focuses directly on a character who, from the very beginning, has been granted special importance. As both Toto's mother and his indoctrinator in cinematic fantasy, Mita functions as the source of the novel's main drama. Her role in support of the extended family is also well established. What this monologue adds to her portrait is the depth that inevitably emerges when one speaks for herself. In particular, the chapter conveys most explicitly the pain Mita endures in order to maintain her image as "supermom," a successful professional, mother, and wife.

One initial observation: since most of the direct quotations encrusted in Mita's discourse come from Berto, Toto, and Héctor, we may surmise that the center of her life is the home. Her work as a pharmacist (*farmakos* = scapegoat) detracts from her home life in at least two senses: it reduces the amount of time she has for her family, and, by highlighting Berto's economic failures, it creates additional tension in their relationship. Toto's inability to measure up to Berto's macho standards also undermines her happiness. But what brings Mita to the brink of despair is the recent death of her infant child. This crushing loss so dominates Mita's reflections that she views everything negatively ("it didn't mean a thing to anybody anyway, yeah, that's the truth, it didn't mean a thing to anybody, and everybody forgot and now it's like nothing had happened" [106]). She can think of nothing else, returning again and again to the moment of death in somewhat exaggerated terms: "the midwife didn't say a thing, it seems what she did do was rush forward and knife me with a scalpel and I hold on to the bars because I don't want to touch my chest and feel the sharp edge of the scalpel, but I can't stand it a minute longer 'there's nothing left to do' she came to tell me, and she carved me up good like a butcher" (110).

Rather than "simple" parody, which characterized Puig's treatment of Choli, this passage embodies a two-tiered significance. First, there is real pathos, the sort evoked when noble, virtuous figures suffer an unjust, tragic fall ("from the highest star, from higher than the stars we fell" [106]). And beyond that, in the choice of grossly sentimental images and language, lies the essence of Puig's uniqueness as a writer. Rather than obliterate entirely the scene's pathos, the *bathos* of the character's discourse merely lends it an unfamiliarly common quality. In essence, this is the idiom of Hollywood speaking itself through Mita, an idiom that is here stylized but not burlesqued. Mita cannot help but articulate these thoughts and feelings, since, in her circumstance of cultural dependency (one certainly not of her own election), they constitute the most sublime mode of expression to which she has access. On such a note of heightened poignancy, the first part of the novel draws to a close.[8]

In the novel's second part, the dominant motifs already noted – mass culture, deceit, power, relativism – continue to prevail in the soliloquists' discourse. A pronounced difference between parts 1 and 2, however, resides in the increased number of male narrators (five) in the latter part, a thematic shift strikingly analogous to the novel's overall narrative shape. Whereas the first part begins in an outgoing, chatty manner (the domestic colloquies) and moves generally toward introspection (the interior monologues), the second part reverses that interiorizing process. The chapters that focus on the unexpressed thoughts of Héctor, Paquita, and Cobito (9, 10, and 11) flow into chapters that represent various forms of the narrator-characters' writing: Esther's diary (12), Toto's essay (13), the anonymous letter to the school headmaster (14), Herminia's notebook (15), and Berto's unsent letter (16). This formal metaphor of phallic extroversion (juxtaposed to its feminine counterpart) reinforces the undercurrent of sexual tension already observed in the Casals family. Achieved by means of eliminating the unitary, authoritative narrator of conventional fiction, this diffuse but pervasive figuration of an unresolved battle between the genders shows the depth and breadth of Puig's commitment to interactive verbalization as a principle of social conduct as well as literary creation.

The drift toward writing (the author's) representing writing (the character-narrators') also brings with it a qualitative shift in the degree of focus on language per se. The styles of each speaker ("speaker" is less literal in the final chapters) become more markedly a pose, a role, a mask adopted for the occasion rather than an aid in discovering the truth about oneself or the world. Rodríguez Monegal's dictum about the novel's estranged language thus applies in certain instances with stunning accuracy. Even the narrators who appear to speak spontaneously (those who do not write) deceive themselves to a large degree as to their personal identities, taking for their own the images and values of some alien other. Curiously, though, that sad scenario is played out through episodes that abound in bittersweet and at times tender humor.

Héctor, for instance, feigns the sort of macho diction that Berto might have wished to hear from Toto. The lines "hairpins, that's the only thing Mari has. I'll just drop her and the party's over, if she keeps pestering me, anyway I already fucked her and if they didn't fuck her before in Vallejos it's because they're only good for jerking off" (118) demonstrate clearly his fascination with the power entailed in casual sex. The feigning reaches a pinnacle when he lapses into the discourse of a typical radio sportscaster (125-26), thereby imagining himself to be both participant and spectator in his own longed-for moments of glory. These raptures are merely compensatory camouflage. Too often Héctor allows signs of sensitivity and insecurity, such as his tears of joy (127) and swells of sadness (128), to show through his borrowed protective coloration. As another example of the invasiveness of alien language, Paquita finds herself suspended between what appears to be a hyperbolic sensuality (we have already learned of her interlude with Raúl García) and a discourse of piety. Her interior monologue takes place in church as she waits in line to confess her sins, a circumstance emblematic of her fundamental moral ambivalence. More concerned about the possible punishment she may suffer than the inherent virtue or vice of her actions, Paquita gives no indication of being aware of the vicious cycle of sin-repent-sin in which she is unwittingly caught.

And Cobito, probably the most disadvantaged of the speakers (he is a poor, fatherless immigrant), compensates for his inadequacies in the most hilariously preposterous way, assuming the identity of "Deadly Joe," a gangster figure in which not even he can possibly believe. Similar to but more extreme in his escapism than Héctor, Cobito goes beyond fantasizing an underworld identity. He attempts to rape Toto (a failed attack he ironically terms "the perfect crime") and plots to put the blame on his Paraguayan friend. But for all his linguistic inventiveness (he constantly puns and plays on second, prurient meanings), he too betrays worries about his health (158), his guilt feelings (161), and his lack of a suitable role model (161). Gifted in cruel and demeaning diatribe, and oddly intolerant for one in so precarious a social position, Cobito embodies the antithesis of the sensitive, even-handed author figure that emerges from the overall text. While a child psychologist might call him maladjusted or neurotic (his runaway imagination leads him to misconstrue his situation), in semiotic terms he suffers from a chronic inability to designate linguistically a verifiable referent.

In the case of the narrators who are represented as writing (chapters 12-16), the matter is even more complex, for writing implies the conscious creation of effects (perhaps including spontaneity and sincerity) as well as the thorny question of literary genre. Esther, for example, writes generally within a confessional mode; Toto, within that of the academic essay; Cobito (or whoever pens the scandalous note), the anonymous "tip"; Herminia, the journal of reflections; and Berto, the friendly (rather than business) letter. As they address their prospective readers, these emitters of messages also implicitly address the conventions of the genres evoked. And conformity with those conventions is not always assured.

Esther's discourse (chapter 12) consists of a dynamic conglomerate of other discourses, some well assimilated and others less so. She mixes the Romantic sublime, Peronist demagoguery, and Christian piety with Toto's uncritical palaver regarding adolescent social rites. At times she addresses her diary as a reader-character (176), other times she is her own interlocutor (163, 172), and still other times she speaks to an absent reader (her nephew Dardito, 164), who will never see those pages. Occasionally she is self-conscious in the refined, circumspect sense (she qualifies and makes more precise her assertions), but sometimes she is simply self-deprecatory. She is at her best, I would judge, when in a fit of pique she blurts out what is on her mind and in her heart. She rants, "not only do you treat him [Héctor] like a good-for-nothing but me like a . . . tart! are you crazy or something?" (176), speaking in as much of her own voice as any of us can ever manage.

Toto's discourse (chapter 13) is at bottom a manifestation of the academic essay, but it is tinged in this case with his passion for cinematic romance and considerable lingering schoolboy naïveté. In essence, the chapter shows how he has found a socially acceptable form of channeling his penchant for narrating films. A similar device becomes a mainstay of Puig's fourth novel, *Kiss of the Spider Woman*, where two prisoners recount to each other film plots both as a pastime and as a means of cementing their relationship. Within this text, however, the chapter's significance lies in its function as a portrait of the writer as a youth. At 14, Toto has come a long way.

And, as a writer and a person, he still has a long way to go. His use of corny figures ("the cobwebs of their nocturnal fears" [186]), embarrassed euphemisms ("Carla avoids her companion's eyes and retires to do her toilet" [187]; "*higienizarse*" [271] in the original), clinical terminology ("the squeezing . . . has provoked wounds under the epidermis" [188]), excessively obvious decipherments ("Carla is white like snow, the symbol of purity" [189]), and the like marks him as still an apprentice in the craft of writing. Yet there are many more felicitous junctures in his developing prose, which generally moves with rhythm and communicates clearly. In what I take to be its straightforward honesty, it is in fact a relief after Esther's strained and precious sophistication.

Relief is also the primary function of chapter 14, the anonymous letter to the dean of students at Toto's school. The relief goes beyond the strictly comic, although there is plenty of humor. As the shortest chapter by far in the entire novel, the segment also provides relief by offering only the slightest challenge to the reader's memory. It provides, moreover, a sort of purgative process wherein the reader is confronted with a mystery and given just enough clues for its solution. The systematic avoidance of conventional climax by which David Southard has characterized this novel is thus somewhat attenuated by the almost immediate gratification available here.[9]

The point is, of course, to discover the identity of the offensive letter's author. Several signs, some of which bear mentioning, point toward Cobito Umansky, the unhappy "gangster" who narrates chapter 11. Some of his expressions, especially "spiritual father," ring suspiciously familiar. He has also already exposed his fondness for pranks and other forms of antisocial behavior. And we know from Esther (176) that he has been expelled from school: revenge in the form of calumny is the motive for his actions. But whether Cobito in fact did perpetrate the misdeed, or whether another set of clues could point just as convincingly toward another suspect, is not of the greatest importance. More fundamental is the notion that any plausible interpretation depends on allowing the passage in question to have a dialogue with other significant textual segments. If there is any meaning either to literature or to life, Puig's structures suggest, it is not to be found like some treasure buried on a distant beach. Significance is not an object but a momentary event in a process, an event that can only be created anew with each dialogic encounter.

Having given up all hope of either finding or creating meaning, Herminia (chapter 15) embodies the descent into a discourse of despair. In brief, although she is both educated and talented, albeit frail of health, she dismisses herself at age 35 as a "common and dreary case of spinsterhood" (199). Her dismal outlook, located at the novel's chronological endpoint (1948), deflects downward the reader's parting view of the fictional world. Paquita, who has found herself a promising fiancé, constitutes an object of envy, while Delia, who has had illicit liaisons with Héctor, is a target of scorn. And Toto, whose evolution is most central to the work, appears bright but is, in Herminia's opinion, a petulant, effeminate, and vain adolescent. Were it not for certain "cracks" in Herminia's discourse, the pall she casts over the narrative might be construed as definitive. Her chief intellectual blind spot is the uncritical acceptance of the term and institution of "spinsterhood." It never occurs to her, for instance, to question why there is no masculine equivalent to the expression "old maid" ("old man" [dirty or not] fails in that regard, for it neither designates the person's marital status nor carries the social stigma of rejected merchandise; "confirmed bachelor" has a decidedly positive ring in that it depicts the male's singleness as a matter of choice). What's more, problems of a logical nature, such as the tendency to digress and to contradict herself, haunt her monologue. But both of those considerations pale before this one: the voice implicit in the novel's overall form speaks here with thunderous force. Herminia's final wish to disappear into eternal silence ("It would be a blessing if death were like sleeping forever without ever again being reminded that Herminia once existed" [216]) collides headlong with the text's established pattern of salubriously problematic verbalization. The nothingness of Herminia's nihilism discredits itself, opening the way for a synthetic concluding utterance of palpable irony.

Berto's unposted letter (chapter 16) inspires in English a meditation on the homonymous pair *mail/male*. The relation between the terms in this context proves to be antithetical, for the social transfer of information ideally associated with the postal service is here shunned by the embodiment of manliness. After unburdening himself of years of resentment toward his older brother, Jaime, his sister-in-law, Adela, and even destiny itself (thereby providing the reader with a perspective long suspected but only now confirmed), the strong and silent Berto reverts to strict conformity with the macho ethic. Real men, in Berto's view, do not confess their doubts and fears any more than they live off their wives' earnings. In fact, the list of don'ts incumbent on Berto's delicate masculinity is too long and tedious to rehearse exhaustively. Suffice it to say, as concerns Toto's chances for paternal approval, that turning into a movie buff and a writer stands as a major transgression.

The Oedipal drama described in part earlier produces the following outcome: the castrated boy adopts the pen as a substitute penis (in Berto's view *pen* and *penis* are as mutually exclusive as *mail* and *male*). The re/dejected boy then authors a tale (the novel) in which the paternal authority figure (the omniscient narrator) is bypassed in favor of a polyphonic array of relatively informed narrators (including most emphatically the inarticulate father).[10] The work concludes aptly by catching the father in the act of discarding his worthless proxy phallus (the letter), an asemic act symbolic of self-castration. This moment of solipsism (dialogue with oneself alone), perhaps the ultimate consequence of Rita Hayworth's treachery, is only intensified by the paradox inherent in its meaningful communication to the reader. From the standpoint of a young, marginalized author, rarely has poetic justice ever been so sweet. Rather than bludgeon his "spiritual father," as his creation Cobito attempts to do in various ways, the author figure has found a nuanced, constructive vehicle for representing his diffidence with regard to authority.

Not the least noteworthy of the nuances in Puig's first construct is the novel's particular shape of time. Largely chronological (from 1933 to 1948), the work suddenly loops back over itself in the last chapter, returning almost to the point of its origin (as mentioned, Berto's letter is written while Felisa and Amparo conduct their conversation in chapter 2). In fact, if the first two chapters were considered mutually contemporaneous, the novel would inscribe an arc in which its beginning and end were the same. But, to his credit, Puig has not succumbed to the temptation to be so tidy. He has broken the pervasive fiction of linear time without falling into the trap of replacing that line with an equally fictional circle.

Circularity, with its closed symmetry and implications of endless repetition, does not suit the gently insurgent forces set in motion in *Betrayed by Rita Hayworth*. More appropriate to the novel's generalized attitude of irreverence toward power is its ambiguous eschewal of geometry altogether. The unrepresentable curve of its shape marks a significant break from the past and a new departure toward a destination as yet to be determined. With this novel Puig announces his entry into a space we might call a "poetics of the pro-saic," a complex of factors that takes as its subject matter what some might see as cultural refuse. More important, however, Puig's poetics features a heterogeneous set of endearing or exasperating but always convincing vernacular voices. As we shall see in the ensuing chap-ters, it is a poetics to which he returns repeatedly while exploring, like a pioneer in a new continent cut off from the fatherland, its pre-viously untapped riches.

Chapter Three

Generic Fiction

Heartbreak Tango and *The Buenos Aires Affair*

In a remarkable story titled "Pierre Menard, Author of Don Qui-xote," Jorge Luis Borges tells of a twentieth-century writer who manages to achieve something not even the great Cervantes could: he writes an original text whose every word replicates those of the Spanish master.[1] Neither an act of shameless plagiarism nor of dark wizardry, but rather one of sheer creative will, Menard's *Don Quixote* demonstrates the ultimate ground of difference upon which a seeming sameness attempts to stand. For however rich and varied may be the meanings spawned by Cervantes's original novel (and they are incredibly, almost limitlessly rich), they pale in comparison to those of the doubled, belated text, born entirely of another culture and place in history. If, as is often alleged, the mad knight of La Mancha's adventures never have the same meaning for two different readers or to any one reader on two different occasions, just think of the incalculable distinctions that arise between Cervantes's and Menard's versions, identical in word though they may be.

From the many conclusions that may be derived from Borges's clever paradigm of radical ontological and epistemological instability, let us isolate just one: not only can't you tell a book by its cover, you can't tell a book (that is, know its identity and encapsulate its meanings) by its insides either. Common sense, bourgeois notions about individual identity as being self-evident, continuous through time, and independent from its surroundings do not stand up under Borges's rigorous postmodern scrutiny. And if no text can be counted on to be equal to itself, it goes without saying that generalizations that try to encompass two or more objects (it matters not whether we refer to books, persons, or bars of soap) can only intensify the problems of knowledge and identity inherent in a single text. Yet in our daily lives we assume we understand phenomena in the world, that we can measure and interpret these phenomena by going from the particular to the general (and back again) without significant effort, and, especially, without thinking. The daunting complexity of the transit between the singular (multiple within itself) and the generic (a multiplicity of multiples) – a sort of obstacle course fraught with hazards and rarely navigated with anything resembling success – forms the underlying pattern of Manuel Puig's second and third novels, *Heartbreak Tango: A Serial* and *The Buenos Aires Affair: A Detective Novel.*[2]

We have already seen how in *Betrayed by Rita Hayworth* Puig mounts an insurrection against paternal authority – an uprising that structures the novel on a variety of levels, allowing for its peculiar consistency and precipitating its most intense dramatic development. In the two novels that follow, Puig's inquisitive, subversive nature leads him to concentrate on another type of authority, but one much less easily embodied in a single, unified figure. This is the authority of received ideas, the trite complacencies and popular myths that permeate existence so thoroughly that one hardly notices their presence, much less their constraining, canonizing force. These hackneyed saws and shelf-worn icons function as the generic frame within which the specific vagaries of contemporary existence are apprehended and evaluated.[3]

Although the two novels differ in many regards, they explicitly invite comparison by signaling in their subtitles association with an established genre (serialized melodramatic fiction and the detective novel, respectively) of mass-produced and mass-consumed literature. Part of Puig's concern obviously lies with writing itself, the forms and styles that reproduce themselves and captivate millions of readers. The extent to which the novels actually conform to the conventions of those genres is the object of considerable portions of the discussion in this chapter. But the notion of genre itself is an abstract one: people read novels all the time, but no one to date has ever seen The Novel. Such a notion can thus be of only secondary importance to the populist Puig, whose conscious interests lie principally in the concrete and the mundane.

Another, more immediate aspect of the authority of received doctrine, evoked in the titles themselves (the "Heartbreak" of the first novel [literally, "painted little mouths" in the original Spanish] and the "Affair" of the second), has to do with gender, the feminine or masculine subclass into which living beings (plants, animals, and language) fall. Puig's characters behave according to models of sexuality (of courtship, conquest, connubiality, and the like) that for a variety of reasons rarely function satisfactorily. Whether searching in solitude for their own sexual identity or engaged in intimate interplay with an expectant Other, Puig's creations often fail to "connect" with themselves or their partners and thus miss the carnal or affective plenitude they assume to be their birthright.

Heartbreak Tango

What aspects of serial fiction pertain to *Heartbreak Tango*? One of the most salient formal features of that genre, of course, is its fragmentariness.[4] Contrary to works that are materially unified in time, the whole is never as important as the isolated effects of its parts. No matter which segment of the serial one sees or hears, the rest of it is always elsewhere, out of view in either some other place or time. For the spectator/reader, there is a sense of unencompassability, of incompleteness, of forgotten antecedents or unforeseeable consequences, and therefore of a frustrated desire for the meaning that derives from a total vision. The motive behind the installments in serials, to be sure, is to titillate receivers' emotions and then cut them off just in time to ensure their return another day, to heighten incidental suspense, and to forestall the advance through an overarching process toward climax and completion. Lest there be any doubt, we are speaking here of commercial, reader-determined writing, in which authors provide within a rigidly preordained framework the sorts of images they believe audiences want to receive, regardless of the text's intrinsic aesthetic requirements.

Stylistically, one may expect to encounter a series of mechanically reproduced cliché images, either on the level of expression (platitudes) or in the elements of the story (characters, scenic components, thematic developments, and the like).[5] The initial "Once upon a time," the discovery of hidden noble lineage in a virtuous pauper, the return home after an accidented journey, and the concluding "happily forever after," once proper to folktales but now reproduced through a plethora of commercial media, are familiar

examples. The lack of discursive variety (reduced lexicon and simpli-
fied diegetic syntax) belongs to a strategy of consumer acceptance
through familiarization. These standardized, transparent devices
tend to engage the mass reader unreflectively in the anecdote. And
to further enhance that readability, such a generically determined
plot is normally rife with melodrama, a register of writing that is
marked by heightened sentimentality and Manichean characterization that tends reductively to order all problems as confrontations
between good and evil. Former President Ronald Reagan's emplot-
ment of himself as indignantly defending the "free" world against the
aggressions of the pre-*perestroika* Soviet Union's "evil empire" (a
contrivance made all the more prominent by the empire's swift dismantling) exhibits all of these elements – fragmentariness, cliché,
and melodrama – at once. We are behooved to be on the alert –
and here lies the special pertinence of Puig's enterprise – that serial
fiction's realm is by no means limited to pulp novels or soap operas.

To recreate the effects of serial discontinuity, Puig has taken
recourse to three main devices. First and most obvious, rather than
"chapters," he has dubbed the novel's sixteen major divisions
"episodes" ("*entregas*" in the Spanish).[6] This prominent and reiterated gesture reminds the reader emphatically of the temporal inter-
mittence proper to the *folletín* (serial romance) paradigm. The
second device consists of strategically placed epigraphs. At the head
of each installment there appear excerpts from the texts of popular
tangos and boleros, all but two of which come from the pen of lyri-
cist Alfredo Le Pera and many of which were performed and
recorded by the already mythified heartthrob Carlos Gardel. These
epigraphs serve as a sort of essentialized objective correlative for the
narrative category in question. If periodic doses of un-self-critical,
sentimental posturing constitute a key element of *folletín* textuality,[7]
then these quotations, which render graphically the musicality of an
already thematically melodramatic discourse, provide the theme song
for each episode of the ongoing saga. The third – isolated but pow-
erfully explicit – element of episodicity lies in episode 13, where a
radio soap opera ("The Wounded Captain") forms the background
for a tense encounter between two main characters, Nené and
Mabel. The way in which the serial drama molds the conduct of the
foregrounded characters – effectively eroding the distinction be-

tween the external and internal fictions – discloses the privilege enjoyed by the fragmented paradigm.

In conjunction with this installment-plan structure, the novel evinces a stiff, almost robotic writing style. Some of the lack of fluidity derives from the strategy of the invisible author-figure, who tends to place documents or textual shards before the reader with only titles, if anything, to help situate the fragment. Like some twenty-fifth-century archeologists, the readers are constantly stumbling on decontextualized and perhaps incomplete artifacts whose meaning they are unprepared to determine with precision. And beyond that, within certain episodes (especially the fourth, fifth, ninth, fourteenth, and sixteenth), by focusing on the five main characters during a given brief period, the narration exhibits a pronounced tendency to repeat, with slight variation, a limited number of formulaic expressions ("without knowing why" [51, 57, 58, 65, 72]; "On the aforementioned January 27, 1938, taking a break in the day's activity" [117, 118, 120, 121]). In this way, rather than seeking variety (of which there is plenty on the discursive level, where the letters, agendas, questionnaires, objective narration, etc., interact), the text emphatically displays a monotonous idiomatic plainness every bit as drab as most of its characters' ultimate destinies.

Where melodrama is concerned, *Heartbreak Tango* appears to deliver quite fully on its subtitle's promise. The motivating force behind the complex yet tightly knit plot is none other than romantic, heterosexual passion. It is passion (or passion's degraded counterpart, lust) that motivates all of Juan Carlos's relationships with women, even to the extent of destroying himself (he suffers and eventually dies from that most romantic of diseases, tuberculosis). It is passion that moves Mabel to get involved with both Juan Carlos and his disciple, Francisco (also called Pancho). Passion, too, moves Antonia Josefa (also called Big Fanny or just Fanny) to give herself to Pancho and, when he deceives her, to avenge her honor by stabbing him to death. And the desire to rekindle a potential passion that never achieved climax drives Nené, some 10 years after the fact, to seek to revive Juan Carlos through her letters. Regardless of the characters' chronological age, boy-girl adolescent love and its consequences constitute the "organizing axis" of their existence (Solotorevsky, 55).

With regard to characterization, as the foregoing tends to corroborate, the novel again conforms ostensibly to its subliterary or
paraliterary model. The creations that populate the fiction, to the
extent that we know them, bare few distinguishing traits. Juan Carlos,
during the 1935-37 period, is a strikingly attractive, illiterate, spoiled,
cigarette-smoking womanizer. Mabel is a cynical, physically non-
descript, promiscuous woman with a comfortable economic status.
Nené is a more gullible, relatively attractive woman who is less well
situated financially. Pancho is a lusty, ambitious, working-class young
man. And Fanny is a poor, naïve maid whose main sources of information about the world are the advice she receives from the lady of
the house and the sentimental films, tangos, and boleros she takes in
through the mass media. Those are the identities with which the
characters are conceived, and that is how they remain throughout
the tale. They are equipped with only the most rudimentary psychological mechanisms and undergo no internal developments corresponding to the changes in their external circumstances. If, as
Borges's fable contends, life is nothing but contingency and process,
Heartbreak Tango appears to have precious little to do with life.
Rather, it evokes a kind of heavily codified and commodified literature – one that limits the flux of life to the movement of inert elements through a time/space continuum. The rigid quality of the style
finds an analogue, therefore, in the simple division and null interaction between the characters and their circumstance.

Respective of a dualistic framework for understanding the world,
again the novel does, at some level, propose such a simplistic
scheme. In fact, it would not be farfetched to characterize the work
as a contemporary narrative version of the morality plays we normally associate with medieval times. Poetic justice is meted out in
Heartbreak Tango with what appears to be an ethical fervor. Since
all the characters, save Fanny, are guilty of one sort of betrayal or
another, all suffer fates as ignominious, or insignificant, as their
deeds. It is indeed noteworthy that the one who suffers most (by
dying both violently and irredeemably) is Pancho, who dares to step
out of his class-determined role by seducing Mabel, the former lover
of his "master," Juan Carlos. And the one granted the greatest
clemency is Raba, who despite her bloody homicidal deed never
contemplates treachery. Puig has been characterized as a utopian
writer[8] – a claim, in that unrefined form, with which I am not

entirely comfortable. Outcomes like this one, however, where the meekest does seem to inherit the earth, go a long way toward explaining the perception of utopianism.

Despite the numerous points of contact between *Heartbreak Tango* and serial fiction, however, it should be clear that the novel is not an apish copy of that mass-produced genre. "Contrary to what the novel's subtitle [*A Serial*] and the word *entrega* in each chapter's heading would affirm," Lucille Kerr has stated, "*Boquitas pintadas* lacks the apparent *sine qua non* of serial fiction. Given that the text's installments are not, in fact, installments – they are not separated by the temporal gaps that would help to produce the kind of indeterminacy typical of the genre – and, given that the reader's appropriation of the text is thus coincident with, but not determined (i.e., postponed or regulated) by, the temporality of publication, as is the custom of serial fiction, *Boquitas pintadas* also renders impossible the identity that its subtitle and chapter headings insist upon affirming" (Kerr, 92-93).

Indeed, the subdivision of the text into a dazzling array of discourses – including a wide variety of documents (agendas, letters, obituaries, mortician's reports, social columns), dialogues, hidden dialogues, streams of consciousness, and hyperobjective third-person narration – and the montage-like and thoroughly defamiliarizing manipulation of the temporal order of the segments manage to unsettle the reader and recreate something similar to the fractured vision proper to serial fiction. But the distinction should remain clear: the temporal gaps built into conventional serial fiction are here displaced to inform the abundant spatial gaps of this "inverted double" of the *folletín* genre. Likewise, the other main aspects of the genre are evoked in such a way as to render impossible the identity between the specific text and the category that text evokes. *Heartbreak Tango* can make the rare boast that it is not "real" sappy corn. Rather, it is imitation kitsch, an amalgam of pseudoclichés with a critical difference.

In view of this unorthodox assertion, consider the following. The stylistic woodenness, as noted, is restricted to a few textual junctures and occurs within a context of unceasing discursive heterogeneity. Even the fragments that exhibit a pronounced descriptive stasis (those narrated in the third person and those that provide answers to their own questions) thus contribute to the dynamic, polyphonic

quality of the text. As for the components of melodrama –
sentimentality, schematic characterization, and simplistic moraliz-
ing – the first two elements apply only to the fiction (the characters
themselves conform to those melodramatic principles) and not to the
text as a whole (the way the fiction is conveyed). The text, through
the machinations of the inaudible yet patently hyperkinetic author,
distances itself from, without rejecting outright, those same melodramatic principles. And the just distribution of rewards and pun-
ishments among the characters (clearly the work of the author-
figure), is even more problematic, embodying a double irony. That is,
Big Fanny "triumphs" in the end (pun appropriately intended)
despite her violently criminal behavior (one incongruity), but only
relative to the other, more insipid characters (another contingency).
Her extremely modest aspirations – a name for her children, a roof
over their heads – dramatize the appalling lack of options available
to these denizens of the provincial everyday. The ultimate value of
the moral judgments rendered in the novel remain, therefore, a
wide-open question.

Rather than an ironclad rule or a sinister trap, the typifying label
acts as a point of departure, of engenderment (*genre* connotes origin
as well as kind) and interaction between the individual and the set in
which the individual fragmentarily participates. Beyond its subtitle,
the novel suggests enough affinities with serial fiction for us to recognize the model easily and to maintain it as a point of reference.
Rather than conform meekly to the mold, however, the text plays
with its axioms, recontextualizing the familiar contours and disrupting automatic readerly associations. At the same time, by subjecting
the standard and banal form to such close scrutiny, the novel implicitly grants it significance and value. It is thus impossible to determine
whether the author's intention is to appropriate the *folletín* as an
object of parody or to represent the influential and popular genre in
a neutral or even appreciative performance of stylization.[9]

Against the backdrop of this profound undecidability with
respect to the generic identity of *Heartbreak Tango*, one finds the
world represented within the fiction marked by an astonishing
quiescence. Puig's creations may differ from one another in social
class, political disposition, professional ambition, and the like, but
they are uniform in the docility with which they respond to the conventions of their station. In fact, despite the sympathy Puig generally

shows toward his creations, it is a hallmark of his writing that the characters often prove to be inferior in perspicacity and circumspection to both the reader and author figures implied by the texts. Not only are they blind to their status as characters, in the Pirandellian sense that applies to a character like Augusto Pérez in Miguel de Unamuno's *Niebla* (Pérez realizes during the course of the fiction that he is a product of the author's imagination and challenges the author to change his fate. Who among us, after all, can live up to those metafictional standards?).[10] In a less literary and more existential sense (akin to the "evil empire" example cited above), they are unaware that their semiotic activity (thoughts, words, gestures, and deeds) reflect their consumption and assimilation of mass-marketed images whose value they never question. In *Heartbreak Tango*, of course, one may attribute this sheepishness to the insular setting or to the dominant ethos of the times (like *Betrayed by Rita Hayworth*, this novel is set in the isolated village of Coronel Vallejos in the 1930s and 1940s, Puig's fictionalized version of the General Villegas of his birth). Whatever the explanation (the later novels move to more cosmopolitan venues, indicating a truly grave situation from which we are not insulated by time or place), however, the characters subsist almost invariably under a burden of alien compulsions whose subliminal spell they cannot break.

The lack of reflective acumen within the fiction is particularly pernicious where gender-specific conduct is concerned. All the characters in *Heartbreak Tango* assume that stereotypical qualities of sexuality apply with the force of absolute and categorical edicts. Deviation from the normative script, which posits a strong and aggressive male in confrontation with a weak and passive female, is not only impossible: it is inconceivable. The prospect of a rationalist, assertive woman or an imaginative, nurturing man, much less a homosexual or bisexual of either sex (these options will be taken up in some of Puig's later works), lies forever beyond the realm of these tradition-bound subjects. As a result, social life boils down to a conflictive interaction with one's mutually exclusive sexual Other, a hostile encounter in which the mobile male seeks an easy conquest while the stationary female attempts to channel the male's desire into a protracted commitment. Availing themselves of complementary, but similarly reductive, behavioral recipes, the sexes vie for a dominance that depends on which one can whip up the more seductive dish.

On the male side of the ledger, despite their apparent differences, Juan Carlos and Pancho amount to two variations on the same tired theme. Both womanizers take their cues from the legendary Don Juan, a character whose sexual exploits have alternately damned or redeemed him since the Golden Age of Spanish literature (the friar Tirso de Molina's *The Trickster of Seville* [*El burlador de Sevilla*] dates from the middle of the seventeenth century). Like the archetype, Juan Carlos distinguishes himself as a "serial lover," one whose personal identity depends on the constant reaffirmation of his potency.[11] His chief identifying features are few and invariably physical: a pretty face and a hyperbolically large penis. Despite his moral bankruptcy (he is a liar, a thief, and a vagrant who greets the news of Pancho's death with a satisfied smile), women tend to look upon Juan Carlos as an erotic savior, a motif reinforced by his Christologically significant initials and the timing of his own death, which takes place during Holy Week. His self-consuming sexuality (emblematized by his compulsive cigarette smoking) encapsulates his "personality" – his mother's, sister's, and lovers' efforts notwithstanding. He enacts, with his every failing breath, the conflation of libertinage and liberation.

More plebeian of origin and less erotically magnetic than Juan Carlos, Pancho has to work harder to meet the conventional standards of manliness. But adhere zealously to that orthodoxy he does, even managing to outstrip his immediate role model in the process. Whereas Juan Carlos surpasses him in the sheer dimensions of his virile organ, for example, Pancho more than compensates by fathering a child with Raba (J.C. has no such issue). Not content with conquering a maid of his own socioeconomic class, moreover, Pancho succeeds in seducing Mabel, thereby achieving an upward mobility greater in magnitude than that of his ailing comrade. It is trite but true (a formulation that frequently applies to the thematic level of Puig's writing) that death is the great equalizer. That both these figures of stock male behavior – one lyrical and the other prosaic – suffer an untimely passing would seem to indicate their essential sameness where matters of gender relations are concerned. Their similarly premature demises could signal as well the wish to attack the root of the problem by burying the macho myth itself.

The featured female characters in *Heartbreak Tango* may approach the question of gender roles from an angle opposite to that of the men, but they are no less wedded to the same set of basic constraints. More numerous than the men (there are three: Mabel, Nené, and Fanny), the women tend to sort themselves along socio-economic class lines. Curiously and significantly enough, the privileges normally associated with each class stand in an inverse relationship to the benefits inherent to each character's fate.

Mabel, the most economically secure and psychically powerful of the lot (she controls the scene with Nené in episode 13 and dictates Raba's behavior after Pancho's death), must endure the harshest of conditions later in life. She is the most cynical, the one who plays the dating game with the greatest opening advantage. She displays a lack of solidarity with both Nené (Mabel continues her relationship with Juan Carlos while he is courting the chaste Nené) and with Fanny (Mabel sleeps with Pancho, the father of Fanny's child, under Fanny's very nose). Later, she successfully lies to the authorities to avoid an embarrassing implication in Pancho's death. For all her cunning and her advantages, though, Mabel does not prosper. For purely economic reasons, she marries a man for whom she has no affection; despite this disingenuous measure, however, she must keep working beyond her normal retirement age to pay for medical treatment for an infirm grandchild.

Nené, in several senses, occupies the middle ground. Less wealthy and assured than Mabel, she believes her only chance to find True Love with Juan Carlos is to resist his advances and, even though she is no longer a virgin, save herself for marriage. She later yields to the temptation to find middle-class security with an unattractive provider, only to suffer a midlife crisis upon confronting the boredom of her drab existence. This crisis precipitates an epistolary drama that involves Nené, her husband, Massa, and Juan Carlos's vindictive sister, Celina – a drama far more interesting than the cliché interaction between the original pair. When the crisis subsides, however, Nené chooses after all to return to her husband and to forsake her fantasy-ridden relationship with Juan Carlos. Caught between a meaningless present and an equivocal past, Nené takes the path of least resistance. Realizing her entire life has amounted to much ado about very little, she determines to sacrifice Juan Carlos's falsified memory on a pyre of insipid domestic tranquility.

Something of an extraneous element in the neat narrative scheme (having no direct involvement with Juan Carlos, who is cen-

tral to all the other characters' motives), Fanny takes the novel onto
a course of surprising ascent. Albeit somewhat twisted, hers is a yarn
of innocence rewarded and of paradise regained. After being
betrayed and abandoned by Pancho, avoided by Nené, and dealt
with heavy-handedly and even criminally by Mabel, poor Fanny continues to hope steadfastly for the day when her prayers will be
answered. Her trust in human goodness, her loyalty, and her sweet
sentimentality carry her through the nightmare of Pancho's assassi-
nation and, unbelievably, on to relatively genteel well-being. Like the
other two women, to be sure, her status depends on her finding the
"right" man on whom to depend – the difference being that Fanny,
whether because of her simple virtue or out of sheer luck (I incline
toward the latter), manages to succeed.

The upswept trajectory of Fanny's *Cinderella* story stands in
stark contrast to the conniving Mabel's vertical drop and the bland
Nené's regressive vacillation. Together they constitute three possible
scenarios of dependency available to women in the convention-
bound world of gender relations. Together, too, they disclose a lack
of freedom in the way men and women conceive of themselves and
conduct their lives, regardless of the social class into which they may
be born. Seen through the discursive prism of the shifting and contradictory relation between the novel *Heartbreak Tango* and its
packaged generic subtitle, *A Serial,* that revelation of unreflective
self-shackling has the force of a heartfelt lament.

The Buenos Aires Affair

The protagonists in *The Buenos Aires Affair* – the artiste Gladys
Hebe D'Onofrio and the art critic Leo Druscovich – may belong to a
world of greater sophistication (they live in Buenos Aires, have
access to advanced study, manage to travel abroad, and undergo
psychological counseling or therapy), but they fail to come any
closer to understanding their own gendering than do the puppet-like
creatures in *Heartbreak Tango*. If anything, their problems are more
complex and less susceptible to solution. If Juan Carlos, Nené,
Mabel, and Pancho interact with the opposite sex like primitively
programmed automatons, they at least do so (or refrain from doing
so) with a wholesome lustiness that remains intact despite the

specter of illness (tuberculosis, cancer, infantile paralysis) in other realms.

Sexuality in Puig's third novel acquires a sickly, pathological cast that has led one critic to view it as "oppressive," something one might be somehow better off without.[12] Puig himself suggests degendering as a radical remedy for the ailing human condition in his novel *Pubis Angelical* (1979), studied in chapter 5 of this volume. But solutions aside for the moment, despite all their attempts at introspection, their formal education, and their involvement in the world of Culture, the characters in *The Buenos Aires Affair* cannot work out an amicable relation with their biological drives. Their failure to achieve peaceful coexistence with this primary force results in disappointments on other fronts as well (notably, their affective and professional lives) and eventually leads to their destruction, either literal or figurative. In the language of Hollywood, again explicitly present in the novel's epigraphic film scripts, these characters are "prisoners of the flesh," victims of their carnal impulses run amok.

One view of the novel might allow for Leo and Gladys to make an ideal couple, their relationship the pornopop perfect match between a violent sadist and a submissive masochist. But this clever abstraction has little to do with the concrete "case" proposed by *The Buenos Aires Affair*. Both characters' problems run so deep as to involve physical and psychological dysfunction. Rather than cancel each other's difficulties, they compound and magnify them, pushing their already shabby lives over the brink of disaster. Together Leo and Gladys constitute a dual example of how not to deal with the relative sexual freedom available in contemporary society. For reasons of convenience (the novel presents them in this order), let us look at Gladys first and her male counterpart later. Once we have treated the matter of their monolithic sexuality, we will be in a position to address the question of literary genres, which in this instance pertains to the way in which the novel posits its own frames for reception.

During what may be called the novel's present time – the period spanning April 1968, when Gladys returns to Argentina after having suffered a nervous breakdown in New York, and May 1969, when her affair with Leo climaxes and definitively unravels – the reader finds Gladys in a deplorable state. She suffers insomnia, nervousness, and headaches, such that she must take ever-increasing doses of tranquilizers in order to function, and then she has trouble being lucid during the daytime. Interior monologues reveal that she suffers nightmares, entertains thoughts of suicide, and considers herself an "inferior being" (104) and, as a one-eyed woman (the result of an attempted rape by a deranged man in Washington), a source or sign of bad luck. Even before she becomes involved with Leo she cannot experience pleasure without destructive pain (in a masturbatory fantasy she thinks "he also hurts and burns that mouth and tears it, and sobbing with joy and pain it is possible to notice that the flames devouring the flesh already reach the bone and the center of the chest where the soul of a one-eyed woman is all curled up" [62]). And once their relationship takes shape, it is clearly predicated on her submission to his will ("God asked me if I was ready for any sacrifice for the love of my future companion. I answered that of course I was, what's more, it would be my pleasure to bend under Leo's will" [114]).

Gladys's debilitated psychological condition is unequivocally confirmed by the events connected with her abduction, during which she is drugged, transported, stripped, bound, and gagged before being raised to a state of semiarousal and then penetrated in the presence of María Esther (that she derives pleasure from this rape shows the severity of her condition). Ensuing events, moreover, principal among which is Leo's depriving Gladys of her first prize in the competition to represent Argentina in the Sao Paulo exhibition, further demonstrate her utter incapacity to control her life or to offer the slightest resistance to his aggressions. By the novel's end, in fact, her ego is so eroded that she cannot go through with the suicide that promises to provide relief from her anguish. Poised on a balcony and peacefully resigned to leaping to her death, she allows herself to be distracted by a neighbor's friendly gestures. Then she can't decide whether to accept a piece of cake or in which apartment to take a nap, before finally drifting off into a chemically induced purgatorial slumber. Although the novel leaves unresolved the matter of her physical suicide, which remains likely, that question becomes at best moot. What is clear is that Gladys's affair with Leo has left her Humpty-Dumpty identity fractured beyond repair.

But how could it have been any other way? In a most telling gesture, the novel provides information, in the manner of a sexual biography, such that the outcome of Gladys's sad saga appears natural and, indeed, inevitable. An echo of the naturalistic "experimental novel" practiced by Zola in late nineteenth-century France, Gladys's life story is marked from its inception by a fateful confluence of heredity and environment. That is, her genetic constitution – examples of which would include her premature and undersized birth (19), her irregular and painful menstruations (27), and her proneness to headaches, nervousness, and insomnia (24, 38) – interacts with the sort of received generic models discussed in regard to *Heartbreak Tango*. She learns from her mother, for instance, to subordinate her artistic ambitions to the mundane demands of her male companion (19, 22). From her father, who admonishes her to avoid looking like a "dog" ("*loro*" [parrot] in the original Spanish), she learns what (unachievable) type of female body is attractive to men (26). These and other parental lessons are later reinforced by formative experiences outside the home, such as her terrified excitement at seeing the true dimensions of a nude male model (29) and the loss of a boy's affection for having beaten him in an artistic competition (27-28).

Sensing her inadequacies, which are at once traumatically represented and magnified by her missing eye (an absence that becomes an object of fascination for Leo), Gladys learns in her comportment with men to be grotesquely conventional – her masochism constitutes a caricature of feminine submissiveness. An extension of her faulty "vision," Gladys's relation to her gendering implies both excess and insufficiency: by placing too much stock in the glamorous myths broadcast by the pop culture industry, she undervalues her worth as a woman. Her taking up with Leo, whom she sees as her potential savior, the embodiment of cultural and sexual power (he is both a prominent art critic and a man with an exceptionally large penis), is thus thoroughly consistent with the portions of her background to which we are privy. With no will or positive sense of self to speak of, Gladys needs nothing short of a Prince Charming to save her from the genetic/generic conspiracy outlined here. Unfortunately for her, Leo has problems of his own.

In fact, Leo's case is even more severe than Gladys's. Raised as an orphan (his mother dies shortly after his birth, his father remains aloof for years), he evinces displaced Oedipal desires for his sister, Olga, with whom he engages in presexual play (mock marriage ceremonies, genital touching [77, 79]). When rebuffed by Olga for fear of paternal disapproval, Leo expresses his displeasure by defecating on the bed (79). As an adolescent he is prone to uncontrollable rages and erections, such that his life comes to revolve about his masturbations, eventually leading him to change his job, his residence, his friends, and the like (89-91). His recurring sexual fantasies tend to involve a conflation of semen and blood, in the sense that his pleasure depends on some form of suffering in the other party, this being heightened in the presence – whether real or imagined – of an audience. Submission or cooperation from the other, on the contrary, inspires in Leo either sexual indifference or outright disgust (82-83). His one attempt at marriage is, of course, an abysmal failure (96).

Like Gladys, Leo's gendering is at once excessive and insufficient: obsessed with sexual desire, he bears a phallus whose hyperbolic size ironically stands for his impotence ("I can't ejaculate!" [126]). This dire portrait is made graver still by Leo's feelings of guilt, both for having divulged sensitive political information under threat of torture and for having perhaps killed a boy he once raped in an empty lot. Leo is a professional success by the time he meets Gladys but shows signs of deep emotional disturbance. As evinced in the hidden dialogue with his doctor (chapter 8), during which his hair-trigger temper almost betrays him, and in his insomniac meanderings (chapter 11), rife with recurring images of degradation and disease, he is a dangerously violent sadist capable of releasing his venom at the slightest provocation. When he is unceremoniously killed in a one-car accident (196), one can only breathe a sigh of relief, for him and for all concerned.

I have dubbed Leo's and Gladys's sexuality "monolithic" because, despite their differences, they kneel together in awe of the mythical powers of Eros. Like so many "moderns," they have absorbed uncritically the commonplace psychoanalytical notion that sex underlies every aspect of human behavior. Within that popular *geist*, salvation, if it is to be ours, depends strictly on the intensity and frequency of the orgasm. Questions of with whom that muscular release occurs or the possible satisfying alternatives to that sort of spasm (to put things as clinically as possible) never enter their field of vision. As a result, what Leo and Gladys unreflectively view as a solution amounts to a serious compounding of the problem. Again, the complementary notions of excess and insufficiency arise: the characters place too much faith in the status and supposed well-being associated with an unrefined sort of gender-linked behavior, ignoring completely the destructive and self-destructive patterns they inscribe or the more salubrious options they might select.

Seen within the overarching context of Puig's iconoclastic relation to figures of authority, *The Buenos Aires Affair* represents an important step in an authorial process of intellectualizing and making explicit what was once barely conscious and subliminal. Whereas his first two novels function within the framework of a Freudian model, sullying the paternal image and undermining the power of gender and genre, this work scrutinizes critically the monolithic figure of Freud himself. This insurrection against the "Father of Psychoanalysis" takes the two-pronged form of (1) a superficial appropriation of Freudian doctrine, in which, on the thematic-characterizational level, all the right questions are implicitly asked and then satisfactorily answered (accounting for the uneasy sense of inevitability I described earlier with regard to the case of Gladys); and (2) a contrary tendency, at the level of writing, to avoid, minimize, defer, or displace *climax,* perhaps *the* linchpin term in the rhetoric of psychoanalysis.[13] In other words, by insistently decentering the reader's epiphany, the text provides a host of alternatives to which the fictional dual sexual biography remains oblivious. The interaction between the subversive textual form and the patly coherent fiction gives rise to a subtle but still impious lampoon of Freudian psychoanalytic discourse.

To speak of tinkering with an established discursive model is already to address the question of literary genre. Similar to what has been said about *Heartbreak Tango: A Serial, The Buenos Aires Affair: A Detective Novel* both does and does not adhere to the generic constraints announced in its subtitle. There is an unmistakable mystery-novel "feel" about the work – an unexplained disappearance, a contrived scene where some crime appears to be happening, a dispassionate, all-knowing narrator who focuses on potential clues. Within the investigative mode, moreover, we can appreciate that Leo and Gladys are not just mental cases but potentially a case for a "private eye" to scrutinize. But where's the detective (if not the very reader)? What crime is committed (Gladys participates willingly in her abduction; the attack on the homosexual was never confirmed as a homicide)? And why does the narrator repeatedly focus on things that either do not happen (Clara Evelia does not see who or what is to her right [7]; a man who would have been happy to see Gladys does not cross paths with her in Washington [38]) or remain just beyond the ken of the characters (twice, for instance, the narrator reveals what the police officer does *not* read while he turns his attention to important phone calls [70-72 and 151-55])?

If *The Buenos Aires Affair* takes to task pop (both in the sense of popular and phallocentric) Freudianism for its facile coherence, it shows no more respect for the rationality proper to detective fiction, which conventionally limits its purview to mere cognition. Conan Doyle's Sherlock Holmes is a successful sleuth, for example, because his utterly rational mind allows him to reconstruct the utterly rational mental processes of the criminals he stalks.[14] But Gladys and Leo, at key moments in their lives, behave "as if someone whispered in their ear" (37, 77), that is, under pressures exerted by forces beyond their rational or even conscious mind. Were they criminals, a different sort of logic would have to be employed to account for their actions. Analogous to Leo's phallus and Gladys's eye, the third-person narrator embodies excesses and insufficiencies (telling us too much about insignificant matters, then leaving gaping holes in the causal chain) that disfigure grotesquely the image of efficient detection associated with the classic detective novel. If the novel's protagonists die (he literally, she figuratively) of frustration for not having achieved the perfect orgasm, its reader, in order to survive, must learn how to get along without the paroxysmic thrill of neatly solving puzzles and tying loose ends. To borrow Geoffrey Hartman's felicitous formulation, rather than a straightforward "whodunit," *The Buenos Aires Affair* may be understood as a postmodern "whodonut," a text whose relationship with the generic model is characterized by a central, essential absence.[15] Rather than accept the model unquestioningly, the novel elaborates an irregular, shifting "frame" whose particular contours draw into the picture the unwitting reader, who by either reading or ceasing to read is duped into "killing off" both main characters.

A third discursive model implicit in the novel also deserves recognition – erotic fiction. One cannot read past the third chapter without noticing the frequency and intensity of the text's explicit sexuality. Whether written or transmitted through other media, erotic art establishes a relationship of maximal proximity between the sign and its receiver. That is, when receivers become aroused by the image, they lose all critical distance, achieving what we commonly call "identification" with the representation (as if it were one and the same as that which it represents) and adopting the role usually played by the common voyeur. Consistent with his supple subversiveness, however, Puig invites readers both to peep at the prurient material and to consider intellectually what that impulse may entail. Through a variety of techniques (extreme slow motion, the privileging of variety over repetition in the manner of presenting ribald scenes, the incorporation of a subjective and especially a female subjective dimension, etc.), many potentially inflammatory episodes are defamiliarized, impeding in readers a naïve suppression of the text's textuality.

The double-edged nature of Puig's writing distinguishes it from what is moralistically called pornography. Rather than imitate Puig's driven characters, one is invited to meditate on the difference between material whose sole function is to arouse the reader and art that may do so while embodying some redeeming social or aesthetic value. It should be clear that *The Buenos Aires Affair*, whose inquiry into the vicissitudes of gender and genre depends entirely on a frank discussion of the characters' passions and urges, belongs to the latter category. That the novel should have been initially censored by the Argentine military government, when its thrust is clearly to undermine simpleminded responses to base images, must go down as another of history's ironies.

Within the common context of waging a protracted challenge against the widespread authority of gender and genre, *The Buenos Aires Affair* differs from *Heartbreak Tango*, therefore, in its embodying a simultaneous superabundance and shortage of both these generic notions. We have seen how its characters, who grant hyperbolic credence to the importance of sex, derive little benefit from their carnal commerce. In a similar manner, its naturalistic underpinnings and its highly developed psychoanalytical and erotic dimensions reveal the detective-novel etiquette to be inappropriately narrow. Yet, lacking a detective, a discourse of rationality, or even a clearly defined crime, the novel fails to measure up to the simple criteria of mystery fiction. Daring to violate our faith in the assumed relationship of truth between titles and the texts they precede, *The*

Buenos Aires Affair reveals itself to be at once much more and much
less than its name would indicate.

Perhaps the most significant development in Puig's third novel,
however, lies in its evocation and recontextualization of the Freudian model, which until now has marked the conceptual limits of
Puig's fiction. *The Buenos Aires Affair* both avails itself of and trans-
gresses psychoanalytic discourse, which in the extreme fails to reflect
accurately the nonlinguistic world and threatens to stifle creative
self-regulation. The deep-seated ambivalence toward psychoanalysis,
which both empowers and constrains, carries over into Puig's fourth
novel, *Kiss of the Spider Woman*. There the motif is developed with
unprecedented explicitness and explosive power.

Chapter Four

Odd Coupling

Kiss of the Spider Woman

As I was preparing a substantially different version of this chapter, Manuel Puig died, apparently of complications ensuing upon a gall bladder operation. The tenor of what follows is in good measure a reflection on the loss of the author as a living object of study.

On 14 May 1990, *Newsweek* ran an article on a renewed concept in American theater, a series of productions called "new musicals", the most recent avatar of "off-off-off-Broadway." This collaborative venture between a local college and recognized theater mavens was touted as a bold initiative that would allow "a radical change, away from the high-stakes crapshoot of producing new musicals on Broadway."[1] The first of the maverick theater's productions was slated to be, uncannily enough, *Kiss of the Spider Woman*, "based on the Argentine novel by Manuel Puig that inspired the 1985 film" (Kroll, 73). My letters of inquiry to both the show's producer-director Harold Prince and SUNY Purchase's impresario, Martin Bell, as to the feasibility of acquiring copies of the libretto of their adaptation, went unanswered. Involved for the moment in other projects, I let the matter rest.

Puig's name next appeared in *Newsweek* some three months later. A jarringly brief entry in the "Milestones" section read "DIED: Argentine novelist Manuel Puig, 57; of a heart attack, in Cuernavaca, Mexico, July 22. Puig's work *The Kiss of the Spider Woman* was made into an Academy Award-winning movie in 1985."[2] Having maintained a periodic correspondence with Puig since 1981, when he participated in a festival of Ibero-American culture at Cornell University, I was shaken to learn via the mass media that an important aspect of my textual relationship with the author was over. It was not till later, however, that another realization dawned on me: if these two journalistic entries were any indication, Puig would be known to future generations not so much for the diverse textures of his unorthodox novels as for a film in whose production he figured secondarily, a by-product of one of his narratives, *El beso de la mujer araña*.[3]

All the ink spilled in representing stock characters, everyday situations, vernacular dialogue, commodified cultural references, parodies of stereotypes, and the like, and what earned the artist a piece of immortality was the chance conversion of some of his words into images on celluloid. As Puig was, practically from birth, fascinated with the world of film (and this novel is clearly his most "filmsy"), there is some justice or at least a twisted symmetry to this eventuality. But to appreciate the consonance of the author's fate is not to understand why this novel – rather than the seven others he published – has transcended its generic borders, spilling over into the realms of film, drama, and, now, musical comedy.[4] What is there about *Spider Woman* that sets it apart, marking it as especially meaningful?

The most accurate and honest answer to this sort of question – one critics nowadays are reticent to ask – is that I don't know for certain. Neither does anyone else, although, as usual, there may be no shortage of opinions on the subject. Success, both commercial and critical, is no less difficult to explain than it is to achieve. It inevitably depends on such intangibles as balance (between tension and release, emotion and reason, action and dialogue) and timing (both within the text and within history), elements that, even if mastered once, do not transfer easily from one work to the next. Of course, the mechanical repetition of one's past accomplishments is probably the surest way to *avoid* producing a valid artistic representation, let alone a masterpiece. On the contrary, the freshness that comes with venturing into uncharted terrain, occasioning the felicitous juxtaposition of disparate elements – what I call here "odd coupling" – seems like a more reliable guideline for authentic artistic creativity. Even then, however, there are incomparably more ways to get lost than to hit the mark, whatever "hitting the mark" may be taken by publishers, consumers, and critics to mean. These considerations notwithstanding, *Kiss of the Spider Woman*, since long before the author's premature death, has stood out (for me, for many of my colleagues, for the public at large) as Puig's most complete work, the one that addresses the issues that haunted him in the most satisfying, integrated fashion. Let us, in an appropriately eulogistic vein, probe the wherefores of its perceived greatness.

I start with the conviction that *Kiss of the Spider Woman* is Puig's most generally successful novel because it is, far and away, his most powerful. My contention is that, whereas his other novels allude to, but eventually skirt, several suppressed and even taboo themes (homosexuality as social practice, revolution as political activity, film as culture), this work confronts these issues in a candid and sustained manner that is likely to have an impact on contemporary Western readers. The topics, "hot" in themselves, interact, moreover, by means of a minimalist technique such that time, space, the number of characters, and other plot elements are judiciously reduced to their bare essentials, thereby enhancing the novel's dramatic compression and intensity. These unique ingredients – the particular signs and the numerous pregnant silences that constitute the text – combine to empower the reader to respond creatively on a number of fictional and psychological levels. The response is particularly acute and significant because, again, Puig manipulates images that touch our collective contemporary nerve. In short, the highly pertinent problematics dovetails precisely with the audacious technique (although the technique is part of the problematics and vice-versa) such that they give rise to a sense of aesthetic and intellectual fullness. All of which, despite or perhaps because of the effort entailed, amounts to an uncommonly good read.

The novel's thematic power base can be thought of initially as a three-legged stool. But in addition to the three strongest explicit motifs – homosexuality, revolutionary politics, the world of film – there is a fourth thematic strand – writing itself – that not only conveys the other themes but interacts with them as well. Through the adjacency of disparate kinds of discourse (Molina's nostalgic cinematic evocations, Valentín's dialectical syllogisms, the impersonal voice of psychoanalytic theory, that of the cellmates' unconscious, a police report), writing acquires opacity and calls attention to itself – a major instance of the "odd coupling" noted above. Each of the main themes is by itself potentially subversive vis-à-vis the dominant ideology – heterosexual, bourgeois, logocentric – of contemporary Western culture. Together they have the potential to function explosively, unsettling mainstream values and practices and, if reading is not yet totally irrelevant to other realms of our cultural life, threatening to destabilize the balance of power in society.

To be sure, this novel is not the first in which Puig has broached these controversial topics. With regard to homosexuality, the quasiprotagonist Toto in *Betrayed by Rita Hayworth* is portrayed as effeminate or sexually ambivalent and barely escapes being the victim of a homosexual attack. And Leo Druscovich's sodomitic violation and bludgeoning of a male homosexual in *The Buenos Aires Affair* brings him so much guilt that it nearly drives him crazy and does eventually lead to his own violent self-destruction. But neither of these episodes is central to the fictions in which they figure, nor is the question of homosexuality developed systematically. *Kiss of the Spider Woman*, however, through two main vehicles – the character of Molina and a series of apparently scientific footnotes that intermittently break the illusion of the primary fictional discourse – removes the issue of sexual preference from its discreet Victorian closet and subjects it to thorough scrutiny.

That scrutiny, to be sure, is far from disinterested. Rather, it takes the form of an apologia and acquires the quality of a defense of homosexuality. Crucial to Puig's strategy for counteracting Western culture's intolerance toward deviance from the "straight" norm is to portray the gay character Molina as sympathetically complex. The windowdresser's eye for the fine details of design, his sensitive identification with the heroines of the films he narrates, his genuine fondness for his mother and his cellmate, and his attempts (largely hapless) at defending himself intellectually against Valentín's cutting ratiocinations all help dispose the reader positively toward this middle-aged queen (*loca* in the original Spanish) convicted of impairing the morals of a minor.

It should be noted that Molina is not just a typical sexual dissident but rather an individualized subject who identifies not so much with women as with the pervasive stereotype of the subjugated woman. Referring to himself as a female ("I can't believe what a stupid girl I am [134]), he refuses to play a penetrative role in his sexual relations and cannot imagine enjoying sex with a man unless the pleasure is mixed with pain and fear (243-44). Men are, according to Molina, serious, responsible, consequential, whereas the other queens Molina associates with tend toward the fickle and feckless, as indicated by their trivial game of exchanging names with those of starlets of the silver screen. Politically inert, socially outcast, lacking in self-respect, untrained in the rigorous methods of Marxian analysis, Molina must somehow marshal his scanty resources to confront the challenges thrust upon him by the State and by his assertive interlocutor Valentín.

To meet those challenges and gain his release from prison, Molina does the only thing he can do. He converts himself into the Spider Woman, the seductive spinner of webs who devours her mate after coupling with him (260). Each film segment Molina narrates constitutes a strand designed to weaken Valentín's resistance and eventually to trap him into revealing the identity of his comrades in arms, data the informant hopes to pass on to the warden. If successful, this treacherous plan – another manifestation of the betrayal motif that courses through Puig's fiction – is likely to alienate Molina from our affection. But it does not succeed, at least not in the form in which it was conceived, for as Molina seduces Valentín he also seduces himself. When, like a Hollywood ingénue, he falls in love with his cellmate and sacrifices his life in order to pass information on to Valentín's revolutionary cohorts, he demonstrates to what extent he has been caught in the very web of allure he fashioned.

A hero(ine) despite himself, Molina ultimately embodies the ragtag vestiges of virtues – valor, fidelity, magnanimity – commonly associated with an earlier age and possible today only in an impure, parodic, mass-mediated form.[5] It is not an abuse of figural language to aver that his characterization amounts to the author's planting a mischievous kiss on the lips of the (male, Western) reader. By addressing the question of homosexuality directly (the love scenes, although carefully constructed so as not to offend, cannot be taken for anything other than love scenes between men), Puig shows his willingness to play with fire. And by according Molina such sympathetic treatment, Puig enacts a revindication of sexual practices whose marginality has only increased with recent historical events (witness the persistent homophobic hysteria pursuant to the AIDS epidemic).

But the novel's vehicle for dealing with homosexuality is not limited to this one character or, for that matter, to the level of fiction where characters normally dwell. In a series of eight footnotes, spanning chapters 3 through 11, the text also explores the same question, but from a radically different perspective. Here we have not a case study in quasidramatic form (as we find with Molina) but a disembodied, erudite voice that offers an overview of some extant scholarship on the subject of homosexuality as it has been studied by the social sciences in this century. Theories by such prominent figures as Sigmund Freud, Anna Freud, Norman O. Brown, Wilhelm Reich, Herbert Marcuse, and Kate Millet on the sociopsychological origins and ramifications of homosexuality are proposed, debated, and, in most cases, rejected, relativized, or countered.

Rather than revisiting clichés about the role of repression, narcissism, paternal domination, maternal castration, and the like in contributing to the incidence of homosexuality, I propose to take a global stance before this aspect of the novel. Most noteworthy from such a perspective is that no single theory or group of theories glossed can explain satisfactorily either the phenomenon of homosexuality in general or the situation of Molina in particular. I do not conclude out of hand from this limitation, however, as some critics have done, that the footnotes function to burlesque psychoanalytical or sociological theory.[6] Instead, I take at face value Puig's comments as to his felt need to disseminate information on the matter, even if the scholarship represented, especially in the area of non-Freudian and particularly feminist psychoanalysis, is far from the last word on the subject.[7] The sort of play going on here, rather than mere spoof, is the endless freeplay of signifiers, as Derrida would put it, or the polyphonic interplay of indeterminately authoritative voices, in Bakhtinian terms. Puig's mistrust of power, and the lengths he will go to in order to diffuse it in his texts, is by now amply documented. But instead of simply playing out that obsession through the risky technique of the footnotes (numerous students have complained to me about how this feature momentarily interrupts their reading enjoyment), the author outdoes himself by introducing in the last entry the figure of the Danish scholar Dr. Anneli Taub.

What makes Taub so important in the context of the quasiscientific discourse of the annotations is that, whereas the Freuds, Brown, Reich, Marcuse, Millet, et al. are thinkers and writers whose titles can be found in the card catalog of any research library, Taub is something of a nonentity. Like Molina and Valentín, she is an invented figure[8] whose "presence" in the footnotes effaces the neat distinction between reality and fiction maintained until that point. Perhaps this roguish tweak of our nose derives from Puig's familiarity with the works of his senior compatriot Jorge Luis Borges, whose spurious footnotes are legion and who even went so far as to invent an author, H. Bustos Domecq, for three books he coproduced with Adolfo Bioy Casares.[9]

Possible influences aside, however, Anneli Taub's fabricated contributions to the scholarship on the issue of homosexuality do attain a privileged status for the license Puig takes in her name. The conclusions attributed to her read at first like a behavioral explanation for Toto's development in *Betrayed by Rita Hayworth*. And her closing remarks, tantamount to an exhortation for homosexuals to organize themselves and participate in the political process, tend to support the course of action Molina finally chooses for himself. This female authority figure, whose name consists of the same number of vowels and consonants as those of Manuel Puig, whose theories encompass the alpha and omega of Puig's novels to that date, and whose very appearance in the text implies the sort of self-erasure at the heart of Puig's ideal vision of power (see chapter 5 of this volume), demonstrates the enormous personal investment the author has in giving priority to a balanced understanding of homosexuality – a priority long overdue on the agenda of Western culture.

Despite Molina's initially apolitical stance, the novel shows that to speak candidly of homosexuality, let alone of gay liberation, is to engage in meaningful political praxis. The text's second high-risk thematic venture is to try to envisage a way for homosexuality to insert itself creatively into revolutionary politics. Now, lest the novel look unduly fanciful and extremist, we must distinguish between North American and Latin American politics. Whereas the 1980s saw a flowering of democracy in such Latin American countries as Chile, Uruguay, Paraguay, and Argentina, the decade before (that of the novel's writing) was marked by a preponderance of brutal military governments whose repressive regimes tended to curtail or abolish entirely freedom of speech and of the press, not to mention their engagement in acts of torture, rape, pillage, and the like. With legitimate movements of opposition banished and forced to move underground, it was not uncommon for educated, sensible young people to associate with guerrilla bands and, indeed, to carry out acts of sabotage or subversion against the government. When caught, these political enemies of the State were of course frequently treated with little regard for civil rights or due process.[10]

The Argentine military dictatorship of the 1970s was particularly savage in this respect, mounting a "dirty war" (*guerra sucia*) that involved torturing, killing, or "disappearing" thousands of citizens suspected of political dissidence. North Americans have come to take for granted the right to criticize their government, and they even (somewhat naïvely) expect the government to defend that right for them. What they are not often aware of, however, is the exceedingly narrow options offered to them by the two-party political system, a system in which Republicans and Democrats are frequently indistinguishable as to the conservatism or liberality of their views. There are even instances of complete inversions from the norm: North Carolina's Democratic senator Jesse Helms, for example, stands clearly to the right of New York's Republican senator Alphonse D'Amato on the question of artistic freedom. Neither of these politicians, of course, espouses guaranteed free postsecondary education or medical treatment, as Cuba's Fidel Castro or Peru's Alan García have done with enormous popular support. Which is to say that the urban revolutionary Valentín Arregui Paz is neither a lunatic nor a legendary figure, as he might be if the novel were set in the United States. He is, rather, a plausible example of the measures many people of conscience were driven to take under the extremely repressive conditions reigning in Puig's homeland at the time.

These distinctions, often necessary when dealing with cross-cultural phenomena, are especially pertinent in the light of Puig's residence in New York while writing this novel. In addition to wanting to discredit the Argentine military in the eyes of the rest of Latin America (the novel was censored in Argentina until the democratically elected Alfonsín government came to power in 1983), it is quite likely that the author also had a North American reader in mind. The film version, in fact, unequivocally speaks to the North American viewer: despite the Brazilian location (Sao Paulo), an Argentine director (Héctor Babenco), a Brazilian leading lady (Sonia Braga), and a Puerto Rican supporting actor (Raúl Juliá), the language of the original soundtrack is English. Notwithstanding the text's lush aesthetic dimension, this is not a work for complacent speculative consumption. It is an instructive exercise in Latin American realpolitik.

As with the motif of homosexuality, that of radical sociopolitical change is one Puig has flirted with in at least two of his previous novels, *Betrayed by Rita Hayworth* and *The Buenos Aires Affair*. Again, on those occasions the author deals with the question only tangentially or allusively. While most of the characters in *Rita Hayworth* are too young, too old, or too preoccupied with the details of everyday domestic life to actively pursue politics in the conventional sense, the promising premedical student Esther does channel her idealism into the Peronist (military populist) slogans she inscribes in her diary. But these sporadic outbursts of youthful zeal lead nowhere and are in a sense neutralized by the protofascist remarks found in Héctor's monologue ("long live the united jerks of my beloved country" [131]). Leo Druscovich's brush with unionism in *The Buenos Aires Affair* is likewise short lived and furthermore at odds with his lust for personal power. Until the advent of *Spider Woman*, in fact, Puig's fiction focuses almost exclusively on the micropolitical, that level where power is wielded over one subject by another, where events are so meaningful to the individual and so trivial to society at large. The sustained treatment accorded to the possibility of a macropolitical solution to human problems marks not so much a turning point (as he never returns to address the question with equal seriousness) as an apex in the trajectory of large-scale political investment in his narrative.

The representative of a certain kind of class struggle in the novel is Molina's cellmate, Valentín Arregui Paz. It would be comforting to brand Valentín as simply a Marxist, but, like Molina, he is too individualized and complex for us to dismiss him so summarily. And like Molina, he undergoes a fundamental metamorphosis. From an initial position of narrowly doctrinaire militancy, he evolves into an ostensibly sensitive, caring person capable of sharing his feelings and thoughts on a nonjudgmental, egalitarian basis. Despite his near reversal of roles with Molina, and contrary to the dominant interpretations of the novel to date, though, I do not see Valentín as a figure of equal sublimity or significance, however formidable a challenge he mounts to Molina's discourse of seduction.

Valentín's secondary status within the fiction derives, characteristically for Puig, from the position of superior power he initially enjoys relative to Molina. Trained at the university level in political science, practiced in the art of Marxian dialectic, and tempered in the forge of physical torture, Valentín thinks and acts with a rigor and discipline that critically undermine ("deconstruct") Molina's sentimentally escapist film narrations. These are qualities certainly worthy of respect, but they do not overcome an inevitable antipathy that stems from, among other sources, the revolutionary's haughty disdain toward his apolitical interlocutor ("What an ignoramus! When you know nothing, then say nothing" [104]). Before long, Valentín's insistence on consistent reasoning cannot help but underscore certain inconsistencies in his own modus operandi, inconsistencies that lead him to reduplicate, within the isolated space of their cell, the very relations of power he has dedicated his life to overthrowing. His inability to apply the high-sounding values of his abstract theories to the simple and concrete situation in which he finds himself erodes his credibility almost from the outset.

To his credit, Valentín becomes increasingly aware of these contradictions and makes a Herculean effort to resolve them. He manages to unblock a good part of his emotions and to admit not only that he cares more deeply for a woman in his revolutionary movement than for the movement itself but also that the woman he really loves belongs not to the movement at all but to the hated ruling class. His acquiescence to coupling sexually with Molina, surely the most sensational manifestation of significant change in Valentín, reflects not desire for his partner but a desire to please Molina and to exchange affection with him on Molina's own terms. Even his readings of the films Molina narrates to him, at first severe allegorical reductions, eventually become more highly nuanced appreciations of the diverse textures of human experience. Valentín's evolution, grossly summarized, runs from an inconsistent dogmatism to a tolerant pluralism, the latter terms bearing a markedly positive charge in Puig's narrative system. But Valentín's sentimental education, financed through a debt not collected in full by his mentor Molina, never becomes the text's primary object of focus.

The contention of Valentín's secondary role vis-à-vis Molina, itself hierarchical in nature, rests on two key aspects of the novel: the dominant subject matter of the footnotes and certain revelations included in Valentín's concluding dream sequence. As we have already seen, the footnotes deal chiefly with homosexuality, the motif embodied in Molina, not with the topic of guerrilla movements of liberation. There is, to be sure, an exception to that rule: one long annotation, located in chapter 4, that represents officially sanctioned (by the Third Reich) publicity material concerning the second, pro-Nazi film Molina narrates, "the superproduction entitled *Her Real Glory*" (82). This note does bear an explicit political message, but not of the sort that would resound sympathetically in Valentín. In fact, it quite severely contextualizes the version of the film the reader receives from Molina.

Instead of speaking directly to any particular ideology, however, the note's primary function is to emphasize the relativity of all ideologies and discourses. Since the character with the ideological hang-up is Valentín (Molina, who can barely muster a consistent attitude, has no pretensions of maintaining anything so authoritative as an ideology), the note serves as a necessary corrective to his obsessive and imperious Marxist cant. In sum, then, by airing the questions most important to Molina personally (albeit in an erudite manner quite foreign to him) or by justifying his nonauthoritarian position in the ongoing debate in which he is embroiled, the marginal notes work to bolster Molina's protagonistic, and even heroic, status.

That still leaves open the matter of the novel's conclusion, taken by some to embody a sort of apotheosis for Valentín, who in a literal sense has the novel's last words. That is, once Molina is eliminated by the urban guerrillas, only Valentín remains as a focus of readerly interest and, especially, empathy. Having been subjected to further torture, which according to the attending physician has produced third-degree burns in the groin area (275), Valentín is mercifully given a drug to alleviate the pain. His morphine-induced delirium shows the extent to which he has assimilated some of the key concepts implicit in the interlude with his deceased cellmate. In touch with his emotions and forthright in his relations with others (he carries on an imaginary dialogue with his beloved Marta), Valentín closes the novel by demonstrating how he has become humanized, spiritually enriched by the process. Let us see where such an ostensibly sound interpretation fails to do justice to the text.

Beginning with the drug-induced state of the monologue, which marks Valentín as Other with respect to himself, we should consider some of the ways in which the novel critiques the idea of a stable, discrete identity underlying such an account. Those burns in the groin area, for instance; are they not the mark of a *castrato*, of a man

who is not (in the conventional sense) a man, of a man who is perhaps Molina, or more precisely both Molina and not Molina? This
contradictory statement, rather than embodying a logical absurdity,
carries the full force of Puig's vision of both the ideal subject and the
sort of intersubjective relations that would constitute the ideal society. When, after making love with Valentín, Molina says "It seemed as
if I wasn't here at all . . . like it was you all alone. Or like I wasn't me
anymore. As if now, somehow . . . I . . . were you" (219), he posits
the principle of a porous, fluid personal identity, one where the
subject is not viewed as an elemental, unassailable fortress. It takes
the form, rather, of an open-ended construct consisting of myriad
influences, prominent among which, in addition to one's genetic
constitution, are the events, persons, images, and words that com-
prise one's environment.

In Valentín's monologue, the instability of such a contextualized
subject is reflected in the protean figure of his interlocutor. At first
taken to be the physician ("if it weren't for your knowing the way
out of here, doctor, and leading me, I couldn't go on" [276]), that
figure quickly transforms into Marta, Valentín's long-standing object
of desire ("Marta . . . where are you? when did you get here?" [276]).
Marta, however, soon blends with an island girl (" 'Can I ask you to
pretend that she's me?' yes, 'But don't tell her anything, don't be
critical of her, let her think she is me' " [278]), who later changes
into an island ("she's lying in the sea and she lifts her hand and from
up here I can see that the island is a woman" [279]) and finally into
the spider woman ("the spiderweb is growing out of her own body,
the threads are coming out of her waist and her hips, they're part of
her body" [280]). This fantastic figure, who appears in a scene thoroughly stylized in the manner of a Hollywood production and who
provides him with sustenance, is of course a hallucinatory version of
the deceased Molina, both quasisubject and quasiobject of the
dream. Through all these metamorphoses, to be sure, Valentín is
talking to no one but himself, but that self is not the same self who
began the dynamic interaction. It is a self that has incorporated
Molina's notion of a commutable, constructed subject. It is a selfless
self, not just in the sense of altruism (though there is plenty of that)
but also that of alterity, of otherness, such that the only trace that
remains of the initial entity "Valentín" are the linguistic signs of his
ventriloquy. Within such a framework, the character is reduced to lit-

tle more than a simulacrum, a name over a void, and the possibilities of his playing a conventionally protagonistic role are accordingly negligible.

Dissident sexual preference and radical political practice are, in the context of Western culture, topics almost certain to outrage or at least titillate. But to what extent can the same be said for film, a medium that is by now not only commonplace but also in some sense superseded by that of video, which in turn is rendered obsolete by the graphic capacities of the personal computer? Are we not in the Age of the Image, where reading is largely replaced by viewing and where life is reduced to electronic impulses that register within the confines of a small, two-dimensional monitor?[11] Surely the representation of the world of film, even in the mid-1970s, could not be expected to imprint sensationally on the reading public.

To appreciate the force of the film motif in *Spider Woman*, we must first specify precisely what kind of films are involved and how they function within the text. The films Molina narrates do not belong to the world of "serious" cinema, to that of a Bergman, an Antonioni, or a Godard. They are, with one exception, grade B American commercial flicks, unashamedly riven with the facile gimmicks of melodrama, suspense, nostalgia, chintzy glitter, and the like. Such films normally have but one appeal: entertainment. They hold the power of spectacle and are designed to distract us from the tedium or problems of everyday existence, but nothing more transcendent than that. Escape from his mediocre-cum-sordid existence is presumably Molina's primary motive for viewing the films in the first place, and it is certainly one of his principal reasons for retelling the films as stories to Valentín during their incarceration (more about his other possible motives shortly). Valentín, for his part, with unlimited time on his hands, listens attentively not because he expects to be edified, but because he seeks relief from the boredom of his sentence.

Failing to qualify as Art, these commercial artifacts lack legitimacy in the world of high culture – that of museums, symphonic concert halls, or traditional universities. And here is precisely where Puig works a neat inversion of the established cultural axes. Whereas the term *cell* in the novel connotes imprisonment and repetition ad nauseam of the same, a configuration with a markedly downward vector, *celluloid* brings with it associations of liberation, of passage into a realm of inexhaustible novelty and difference. Escapism is not disparaged out of hand. On the contrary, it is studied detainedly, in depth, with an eye to its less-than-obvious complexity, its motivations, its unforeseeable effects. In short, then, what is remarkable about the treatment of film in *Kiss of the Spider Woman* is not so much its presence in the text (a mere reflection of the superabundance of passé technology in postindustrial society) as the unpretentious nature of the examples provided and the unflagging respect that attends their narrative representation.

If escapism serves to motivate the cellmates to start narrating the films, it is certainly not their only reason, nor does it continue for long as their chief purpose. Although the reader is not aware of this level of meaning until chapter 8, Molina has another sort of escape in mind, for he has made a deal with the warden to wear down Valentín's resistance and extract information about his comrades' whereabouts and planned activities. Poisoning the revolutionary's food is one means toward this end, but Molina's preferred tactic is to gain Valentín's confidence. The film narratives are thus designed to promote a sinister, one-sided intimacy (the spider woman scenario): the gay yarn spinner would appear to reveal his feelings, values, and memories, and the pliant guerrilla would be conned into revealing political secrets of utility to the authoritarian State.

Molina's downfall occurs because the above plan works too well. Not only is Valentín's physical resistance eroded, he responds to Molina's invitations to intimacy by uncovering elements of his own psyche that Molina finds irresistible. Here at last is a "real man," the kind Molina has been searching for all his adult life! Once Molina realizes he is in love with Valentín he must revise his objective: rather than relay information to the warden in order to gain his own release, he must play a stalling game in order to stay in Valentín's company as long as possible. He must not elicit information from Valentín, lest he betray both his love and himself. The film narrations continue through the second half of the novel almost as intensely as in the first (approximately 84 pages in part 1 as opposed to 57 pages in part 2), but their function and meaning undergo a drastic transformation.

For Valentín, the change – lacking an analogous ethical reversal – is less radical but still significant. From an inconsequential pastime, the films evolve into the matrix for an almost primal experience.

Through their narration and discussion Valentín reawakens to aspects of life – the joy of eating, of erotic imagining, of intimate sharing, of crying – he had allowed to wither and almost die. After Molina dies in attempting to make contact with Valentín's band of subversives, Valentín wonders whether his cellmate acted out of political conviction or just in emulation of Leni, the heroine of one of his narrations. He never learns of Molina's duplicitous collusion with the State and so never fully understands the irony of his miraculous rebirth. The new meaning he finds in life comes about through his exposure to an illusion, or a series of illusions on a variety of planes. These include the patently idealized films, which are filtered through Molina's memory, then translated into language, and finally are received under a set of assumptions not shared by both parties. Rather than undermine the value of the narrated movies, however, such dynamic equivocality attests to the importance of such mass-cultural objects as a force in contemporary life. By incorporating the rudimentary structures of the films into the nuanced and shifting structure of the text, Puig both legitimates the marginalized artifacts and implicitly questions the boundaries of serious literature.

Some of the ways in which the dominant motifs of homosexuality, revolution, and film interact should by now be obvious. Homosexuality is treated with a candor that, within mainstream society, is outrageous. The seductive power of Molina's discourse is such, moreover, that it invades the space of Valentín's discourse (even as the other discourse impinges on it as well). Revolutionary politics becomes sexualized, sexual dissidence becomes politicized. And the narration of film proves to be a crucial vehicle for sexual-political change in both directions. The cultivation of an aesthetic sensibility within a doctrinaire Marxist, of course, may not satisfy many militants on the left, but the idea that an effeminate gay male could achieve such humanizing results through the use of passé commercial films qualifies as nothing short of startling. And Molina's ultimate determination to act in a politically subversive (though still romantic) manner is no less noteworthy. Puig has always held out more hope for gains in the micropolitical, intersubjective arena than in the national or global theater of macropolitics. But for Puig, unlike Jean Baudrillard, the social is not dead; social progress is still conceivable.[12] Freedom and justice come about, however, not through mass mobilization (which leads to dangerously high concentrations of power)

but with and in one interlocutor at a time, one viewer at a time, one
reader at a time. Perhaps it was Puig's appreciation of the pivotal
role of even the humblest individuals in society that moved the
author to adopt the minimalist technique he so successfully wields in
Spider Woman.

At a time when it looked like the Latin American novel was in
peril of painting itself into the exuberant but ultimately confining
corners of the neobaroque or of encyclopedic metafiction, Puig
championed the refreshing current move away from "literary language." His styles, or lack of them, at times reminiscent of Barthes's
degree zero of writing, work at reconnecting fiction with the worldly
context in which it is produced.[13] In *Kiss of the Spider Woman*,
however, while maintaining his allegiance to plain parlance and
popular myths, he achieves a maximum of economy and efficiency in
the structure of the fictional universe itself. As we shall see shortly,
temporal and spatial coordinates, as well as other plot elements, are
reduced to the barest of essentials. But these economies are
insignificant in comparison to the constraints introduced with regard
to narrative technique: there is none. That is, the figure of the
narrator itself, long considered an indispensable component of narrative fiction, is eliminated altogether.[14] Puig's regard for the unem-
powered manifests itself in an aesthetic of spareness wherein less is
more and thinking small is its own reward.

Spider Woman is, after all, an exceedingly simple tale. With
counted exceptions (the warden, a guard, a shopping list, a police
report, the footnotes), the novel depends on only two characters
talking to move from start to finish. And even though the themes of
their conversations range widely in time and space, the coordinates
of the action are limited almost absolutely to the restricted space of
their prison cell and the weeks or months when they occupy it.[15]
Props consist of little more than the characters' clothing, some
sheets and towels, the food Molina manages to bring in, their beds,
the bars that enclose them. With no narrator to provide background
information or even stage directions, reading difficulties can arise.
When, for instance, Valentín in a fit of pique throws their prized
marble cake on the floor (193), it is only through the reader's infer-
ence that the action can be said to take place.

The scene in which such significant silences play their most capital role is, of course, the first of the cellmates' love scenes (218-19),

but the use of the almost-blank space (graphically rendered as "– . . .") is certainly not limited to moments when words might be offensive or too graphic for the lyrical nature of the scene. They appear throughout the text (see 9, 96, 180, 276, and passim) and, as in much contemporary fiction, invite the reader to participate actively in the completion of the fiction, to "write" it into coherent signification. In addition, the particular junctures where the fissures appear seem to indicate an awareness that language, so important in life and definitely no less crucial in literature, is really not adequate at the peak moments of either. Language is troping, figuration, approximation, not the "thing itself" it tries to represent. At any rate, the presence of so much silence in this colloquial text further supports the hypothesis that Puig's writing, despite the lush embroidery of some of Molina's descriptions, inscribes a logic of austerity.

To say that the reader must function as a coauthor is to evoke Cortázar's figure of the "lector cómplice" (accomplice reader), by now a critical commonplace in contemporary fiction.[16] In view of the critique of power Puig articulates in *Spider Woman*, however, the reader must be seen as more than routinely engaged in a collaborative interpretive act. The reader here constitutes an utterly crucial link in a social transaction begun with the author and transmitted through the text. Nonfeasance on the reader's part aborts the process entirely, not only producing nonsense but also reinstalling the despotic power structure in its place of comfortable dominance. Let us look at this transaction in some detail.

Within the text, two sets of transactions are set in motion, one between the two main characters and another, on a discursive level, between the discourse of oral fictiveness (the "main plot") and the discourse of written scientificity (the scholarly footnotes). Despite their considerable differences, what these textual debates have in common is their tendency to blur the distinctions between what are normatively taken to be binary opposites. We have already established the ways in which Molina and Valentín come to partake of each other's personal identities, such that they merge, acquire some of each other's traits, share dreams, and the like. In similar fashion we might demonstrate the "truth" conveyed through fiction (not a terribly controversial notion) and the fictionality of writing within the domain of the humanities (perhaps less immediately apparent but, as the work of Hayden White and Dominick LaCapra indicates,

still easily demonstrable).[17] In both cases we observe an interpenetration of formerly distinct conceptual fields, with a more nuanced
and dynamic understanding of the overall configuration. Higher on
Puig's agenda than this appreciation, however, is the removal of
power from one pole (the "scientific" one, in both Valentín's Marxian sense and the scholar's psychoanalytic sense) and an equitable
redistribution of forces over the entire field (now properly called
"fictive/scientific" or simply "narrative"). The newly transformed
structure of power now grants as much validity to fiction (Molina's
film narratives, the novel's entire imaginary dimension) as to what is
conventionally thought of as nonfiction.

Something analogous occurs between the reader and the text.
Conventionally conceived of as separate from the text and relegated
to a subaltern, passive role, the reader of *Spider Woman* is invited to
reflect upon several heady matters. First are the ways in which the
reader is in the text (as Valentín, the listener, and as Molina, the
unauthorized speaker, for instance) and the text is within the reader
(the stock gambits of Hollywood films, along with Molina's familiar
emotional responses; the identifiable fragments of Marxian orthodoxy as well as Valentín's predictable turns of logic). In addition,
there is the question of how this mutual interpenetration of text and
reader empowers the reader to respond creatively to the text (to
imagine love scenes, to fathom Molina's motives for sacrificing himself, to write an ending to Valentín's concluding dream sequence, or
to choose not to do any or all of these things). By responding creatively, rather than merely determining the meaning of the text for
him- or herself (thereby "consuming" the text as the commodifiers of
art would prefer), the reader/text realizes the networking potential
of the liberated (autonomous but interconnected) subject represented and sanctioned within the text/reader. In short, to read *Kiss
of the Spider Woman*, internalizing its structure, is to subscribe to a
utopian program, a self-effacing, quasimystical process where one is
prodded to imagine a secular, nonalienated state in which world and
word recouple oddly and flow through each other like (troping
unabashedly) warm salted butter and sugar syrup.

That recipe may be too high in cholesterol and calories for some,
but there is no question that the images and ideas represented in
Kiss of the Spider Woman have made a deep impression on our col-

lective psyche. Again the question arises: why? Have we gotten to the crux of the matter? Convinced we have not (nor will we ever), I suggest (vainly) one more possible explanation for this work's singular importance: death. Not the mere incorporation of this universal motif in the text but, again, the procedure by which the theme is transmitted. Death in the novel, to be sure, is always "out there," lurking beyond the prison bars as a threat against those who challenge the given social order. It is the ultimate coercive force, one that Molina and Valentín are dedicated to resisting by forming an oasis of solidarity within their cell.

As you read this novel, in which unarmed individuals are pitted against the mammoth powers of the State, you have to suspect that one or both characters is eventually going to meet with death and that their storytelling, much like that of Scheherazade in the *1001 Arabian Nights*, is designed mainly to defer that inevitable encounter. But when the expected happens, and Molina finally perishes, you are not accorded the finality you have come to associate with death. Rather, you are given a set of equally plausible choices as to Molina's motives, choices that span the heroic and the bathetic, and you are then assured that his reasons are "something only he can know, and it's possible that even he never knew" (279). Likewise, you are kept in the dark about Valentín's death. Are the (remarkably upbeat) words with which the novel ends the words with which he terminates his earthly existence? Does he live on in order to be tortured again, in a repeated enactment of death-within-life? Or does his newfound sensitivity move him to confess to his torturers? In any case, death is a latent presence that never quite crystalizes, a specter, an enigma or question rather than an entity or answer.

These reflections on death as an ongoing process and an insoluble human mystery arise within the context of another "death," that of the narrator. Far from tragic, the death of the narrator is a ritual sacrifice necessary to the destabilization and reallotment of power within the text, so that other, less authoritative voices (narrators in their own right) may be heard. It is therefore a silence and an absence that engender a deferred meaning, however decentered and disunified the textual surface may appear. That death, of course, dwells in the shadow (now, for us) of the death of the author, the biological, historical subject who will write no more. Perhaps the oddest coupling of all is the marshalling of so many images of death to constitute a work that amounts to a celebration of vitality ("this dream is short but this dream is happy"), a work whose signifying life has only just begun.

Chapter Five

Inscribing Erasure

Pubis Angelical and *Eternal Curse on the Reader of These Pages*

A recent essay on the figure of the author in and around Puig's fic-tion coins the term *dis-appearance,* by which is meant an unconven-tional, self-negating sort of self-presentation by an authorial figure, such that he both appears and disappears in the same gesture.[1] The formulation strikes me as highly felicitous, for it gets at the heart of the subtlety with which Puig addresses the notions of being, social interaction, and writing. For Puig, truth, art, and the truth of art lie in the realm of polyphony, of ambivalence and indeterminacy. To rep-resent such tendencies and values with even partial adequacy, every proposition must entail an element of its own negation, a subtraction or fading intrinsic to itself. To put it mildly, these qualities are not universally appreciated in the dominant strata of Western culture.

The notion of erasure surely does not start for Puig in the novels figured in the title above. He has searched systematically for alterna-tives to monologism, mere assertion, or hegemony (call these *machismo,* phallocentrism, or authoritarian narration). Erasure can be shown to pertain forcefully to major aspects of all his early fiction: to the paternal figure in *Betrayed by Rita Hayworth,* various literary and cultural clichés in *Heartbreak Tango* and *The Buenos Aires Affair,* and a wide variety of commonly accepted boundaries (those between hetero- and homosexuality, self and other, politics and aes-thetics) in *Kiss of the Spider Woman.* In Puig's fifth and sixth novels, however, the motif of erasure plays a role whose pervasiveness is unrivaled in his earlier works. On a number of levels it is made explicit, foregrounded, "thematized" as a process, and explored in its diverse forms and consequences. In this sense, then, the works in question show themselves to be in good measure "about" erasure as a means to constructing a self, a society, and a text. Far from the simple act of expunging unwanted signs (which might at first blush appear to constitute a semiotic loss), erasure in the more recent texts attains the status of a distinguishing feature – and a particularly rich one for the purposes of generating meaning.

Erasure as an operation cannot happen in a single step. It always implies a prior marking, traces of which inevitably remain in some form despite the attempt to delete them. Such a deletion tends to take the form of a rewriting that, while differing from the initial inscription, somehow eclipses without entirely nullifying it. The residue of the original ciphers remains, revealing at least one additional level of meaning. More important, though, the vision-and-revision procedure discloses a history of desired and incompletely achieved silencing by certain agents of repression. In Puig's novels these agents quite often act within a social, political, historical, or economic space, as with, say, anxious parents, prison officials, aggressive individuals, or purveyors of propaganda and advertising. More and more, however, Puig seems to be gesturing toward the inner, psychological manifestations of these forces – the obsessions, complexes, and hang-ups that dictate how we think and act, foreclosing our personal freedom before external inhibitors can even come into play. By insistently inscribing erasure in *Pubis Angelical* and *Eternal Curse on the Reader of These Pages*, Puig exploits the fruitful dynamic between the simply written and the equivocally written-to-be-unwritten-and-rewritten.[2] In so doing, he both textualizes the human concerns that have informed all his fiction (showing how they are implicit in narrative discourse) and extends the somewhat esoteric questions of writing and reading into highly pertinent realms of everyday existence.

Pubis Angelical consists of two chief modalities of writing, one markedly mimetic or realistic (those sections, set in the present, ostensibly pertaining to the character Ana, her dialogues with her friends Beatriz and Pozzi, and her diary entries) and another highly stylized and imaginary (those sections that deal, in the past, with the Mistress/Actress and, in the future, with W218). My method for showing the diverse levels on which erasure functions within the text will be to consider two passages from each modality (a conversation between Ana and Pozzi and one of Ana's diary entries, on the one hand; an excerpted narration regarding the Mistress/Actress and another respective of W218, on the other). A more conventional investigation into *Eternal Curse* will then enable us to see both the extent to which the tendency to write through eradication characterizes Puig's textual practice during this period (the novels were originally published in 1979 and 1980, respectively) and the shades of difference in the way each novel manifests that tendency.

Pubis Angelical

-You can't seek to have access to Lacan any other way. The terminology is important. Otherwise one trivializes it. You are trivializing it.

-. . .

-And that about how the unconscious is the other, the Other with a capital "o," I don't know if you'll remember.

-No, that you never explained to me.

-Yes, of course I did. He says that the "I" is that part of the self over which each one has control, that is, the conscience. Later that part over which one doesn't have control, or let's say the unconscious, passing as foreign, crosses over to join the surrounding universe. It is the Other.

-I follow (in the original, "*Seguí*" [Go on]).

-And part of the Other, of the foreign, is really yours, although that part of you is actually foreign to you, because it's beyond your control. And at the same time, your entire view of the universe is filtered through the unconscious. And thus part of your self is foreign to you, but the entire universe is a projection of yours.

-It's confusing.

-Not really. Always two things in play, do you follow? That's why according to these theories you're never alone, because within one's self there's always a dialogue, a tension. Between the conscious "I" and the Other, which is, we would say, the universe. (147-48)

This dialogue fragment from *Pubis Angelical,* between the 30-year-old Argentine exile Ana and her exlover Pozzi, takes place in a Mexican hospital some time during 1975. Pozzi is summarizing for Ana some highlights of a seminar they both attended in Buenos Aires on the (post-Freudian and linguistically informed) theories of the French psychoanalyst Jacques Lacan. As we have already looked at some of the political significance of Puig's abundant use of dialogue in *Betrayed by Rita Hayworth* and *Kiss of the Spider Woman* (foremost among which are the anticipatory erasure of the impossibly knowledgeable author figure and the provisional empowerment

of normatively marginalized voices), let's look at some of the other
features intrinsic to the passage. We should pay special heed to the
blurring of distinctions between two sets of terms that may be uncritically taken to constitute binary opposites: the self and the Other,
and man and woman.

The pair of concepts most explicitly evoked in the passage is of
course that of the self and the Other, and we may take Pozzi's version of Lacan's model (reductive though it may be) as a paradigmatic
subversion of simple binary thinking.[3] Just as the self (the human
psyche) contains that which is alien to it – the Other, the unconscious, the universe – nothing in the universe is simply itself but is
rather different from itself to the extent that it contains its own Other
as a condition of its being. Put simply, the most basic of algebraic
equations, $A = A$, does not obtain, for it is both true and not true at
the same time. Now, clearly such an assertion runs counter to common sense and would seem difficult to maintain as the guiding logic
for an entire text, much less a philosophy of life. Yet the dialogue's
immediate context provides a concrete example of how such an
abstraction may apply to mundane existence. The conversation
occurs in a hospital because Ana has been interned for severe chest
pains – pains diagnosed as lung cancer. In addition to representing
for Ana the frightening prospect of a premature death, the cancer – produced in her own body, by her own cells – embodies that
Other (neither she nor not-she) proposed in Lacan's theory of the
self. The use of so deadly an illness to represent a condition necessary to one's personal identity may seem extreme. But as a metaphor
the figure of such a malignancy does have the virtue of conveying the
mortal blow such a logic seeks to deal to the conventional notion of
a stable, self-present subject.

Such considerations, however, focus only on the "content" of
the utterances in question. A glance at the passage's form, specifically the characters who deliver the particular lines, indicates
another pair of concepts that warrants critical scrutiny. The one who
pretends to master the knowledge, the one supposedly capable of
reproducing it (even though both participated in the same seminar)
is Pozzi, the male. Ana, for her part, listens meekly, trying to understand and refraining from contradicting his allegations, demonstrating thereby the Lacanian tenet that the self is defined through a

transaction with the Other. The tendency to grant credence to the hackneyed contention that men have a monopoly on scientific knowledge, and to relegate women to a powerless sphere of passivity and affective response, is, for much of the novel, perhaps Ana's most characteristic trait.[4]

Such rigid assumptions regarding gender roles are clearly also operant where politics, the theme of most of their chats, is concerned. In Argentina, Pozzi is a subversive, a defense attorney for political prisoners. He has come to Mexico to convince Ana to lure her former suitor, Alejandro, there, so that Pozzi's band of leftist Peronists can kidnap him and exchange him for an imprisoned comrade. Ana's part in the scheme would be that of the classic siren, a Mata Hari whose charms might be exploited for political ends but whose task would be delimited as purely seductive. To her credit, it is a part she ultimately refuses to play, opting instead to question the hallowed dividing line between the sexes.

Likewise, as the leftist Peronist term indicates, Pozzi's stance enacts a subversion of traditional notions of political mapping. (A military leader who openly admired and supported Hitler's and Mussolini's fascist regimes during the Second World War, Perón was a populist leader whose power rested with the labor unions and a co-opted nouveau-riche bourgeoisie.) A leftist Peronist is actually no more oxymoronic than a politically committed female: the formulations merely encourage us to examine the extent to which the constituent terms are not mutually exclusive. But Pozzi's subversiveness remains on a level that is strictly macropolitical: he dies without realizing the regressive, dualistic nature of his (micropolitical) relationship with Ana.

She, on the other hand, survives her bout with the enemy within (eradicating both her cancer and the self-imposed limits on her possibilities), opening the way for a more lucid and nuanced understanding of herself and her relationships with others and with the world. This outcome, too, is somewhat attenuated by the Hollywood-style finale by which it is conveyed (a hypothetical embrace shared by Ana, her mother, and Ana's daughter). But for the purposes of our analysis, these are the basic challenges Ana must face. The second passage we consider represents something of a midpoint in the process of meeting those challenges.

> And the truth is, I don't think that Fito would have wanted to annoy me,
> he really believed the business of the executive meals was important. I was
> the one to blame for not telling him what I thought. And that's where the
> bile began to collect. There's nothing worse than not talking. But for me
> when something makes me angry I just freeze up and that's all. Maybe
> that's the difference between men and women, that the woman is all
> impulse, all sentiment, and allows herself to be consumed by rage, instead
> of saying what she thinks. But the truth is . . . at those moments I can't
> think. When someone is telling me what to do I don't think. The blood
> rises to my head and that's all. A typically feminine reaction. By contrast a
> man, when someone tries to boss him around is exactly when he rises to
> the challenge. That has to be recognized, that one is born that way. Beatriz
> says that that's not the way we're born, that's how we're trained to be. I
> think it's a matter of temperament. (76)

This excerpt from Ana's diary, lifted from the third of five such
sections, still belongs to the text's mimetic register. While harkening
back to major portions of *Betrayed by Rita Hayworth*, whose final
five chapters consist of characters who represent themselves through
writing, the entry catches Ana in a characteristic pose, that of
reflecting upon herself, particularly her past self, to try to understand
who she is. She is convinced she is a failure. Her method for arriving
at that definition is to ask where she went wrong with regard to her
marriage, her health, and her general way of being.

The passage exhibits both a courageous determination to arrive
at a clearheaded assessment of her condition and, along the way, a
frustrating mystification regarding the questions entailed. Rather
than blame her former husband, Fito, for relegating her to the role of
the charming hostess for his influential clients, she generously
shoulders the responsibility for remaining silent despite her dissatis-
faction. This astute evaluation of her former self-effacement is dulled,
however, by the unmotivated move from her own case to that of her
entire gender.

In portraying her emotional outbursts as typically female, more
than typecasting herself (which she undeniably does), she typecasts
all women. Her tendency to think about women in stereotypical
terms (not taking into account her social class or her entire society's
dependence on Western European and North American values and
icons, for instance), not unlike the cinephile Molina's tendency in
Kiss of the Spider Woman, finds perhaps its apotheosis shortly
thereafter in the line "a woman who doesn't lose her head over an

item of high fashion just isn't a woman" (80). Men, on the other hand, with their rationality and occasional bravado, are for Ana (here one hears echoes of Gladys in *The Buenos Aires Affair*) serious and "superior." Superior to whom is a point of confusion for her, however, for if Ana were truly inferior she would have no hope of attracting such a man ("a superior man, let's say, not superior to me, because then Beatriz would be right, and she's not right, but superior in another sense . . . Well, I'd better start again" [77]).

Her disposition toward either/or thinking in general manifests itself as well in her reported debate with Beatriz over the question of nature or culture as the cause of the supposed gender differences. Ana's stance in the debate is, to be sure, stodgy and conventional. More to the point, however, it is *essentialist:* it posits for both genders a discrete transhistorical, transcultural essence that severely limits the options available to either gender. Without knowing it, Ana has trapped herself within her own preconceptions.

But Ana is nothing if not persistent. Her will to knowledge, as George Yúdice has observed, is every bit as strong as Molina's will to pleasure.[5] When Elías Miguel Muñoz says that *Pubis Angelical* "marks a blurring of 'the feminine' and 'the masculine' as these concepts have been defined in the dominant discourse," it should be understood that such a blurring comes about only after an arduous and protracted struggle.[6] As with Ana's attempt at articulating with consistent reasoning a concept of the superior man, her quest for self-understanding leads her again and again into contradiction ("I'd better start again").

Near the end of her final diary entry she declares, "I must admit that I don't understand anything about what's going on, neither to men (in the original, *ni a mí* [neither to me]) nor to others" (199). Her quest in search of her self is a failure. Or is it? What about her insights into Beatriz, with whom she achieves a new level of honesty? What about her revelations concerning Fito, Alejandro, and Pozzi, men who imposed their will on her to achieve their own personal objectives? What about her assessment of the superficiality of life in Buenos Aires from the perspective of Mexico? What about her decision not to subordinate her mother's and daughter's safety to Pozzi's political aims? She certainly does not achieve the (utopian) goal of total self-knowledge, but surely she makes some considerable gains.

What's more, she recognizes the gains she has made ("But I don't pretend anything, I don't pretend to understand anything, I'm resigned to the luck I've had, that this very dangerous operation that they've performed on me had very good results" [199]). That she has emerged scarred but undefeated from the surgical operation is important but not sufficient. More significant for the rest of her life is the dangerous operation she has performed on herself through hard introspection and self-criticism. And her gains, most emphatically, come about through the destabilizing of the sort of fixed notions evoked in the passage above.

The conditions of her incompletely achieved self-knowledge, cast in purely rational and conscious terms as they are, moreover, need not be regarded as unassailable. Here is where Puig's insistent avoidance of omniscient narration plays a major role. As the narrator of her own memoirs, Ana has access to only part of her identity (an identity that, through her search, she constructs as much as discovers). The reader, on the contrary, may be privy to all Ana learns about herself as well as to her unconscious, her Other. This unreachable side of Ana is the site of at least two freedoms: it is free to organize itself according to a logic other than that of causality; and, even within causality, it need not be constrained by the plausible, where psychological motivation or social interaction is concerned. Let us turn to the novel's symbolic and imaginary sections to see how erasure is implicit in the kinds of meaning and knowledge they provide.

> The Mistress felt Theo stroke one of her hands and afterward hold it gently, she didn't withdraw it, she didn't know whether it was from fear or something else, "I am a Soviet spy. Those who give me orders suspect you to be an agent for the Third Reich, but I'm sure that it's not so, that you fell into a snare set by that dreaded armaments maker through who knows what devices," "You're not mistaken. I'm innocent." Theo took her other hand, "I don't have any evidence of one or the other, but . . . I've . . . fallen hopelessly in love with you, I've lost all my defenses, I'm entirely at your mercy . . ." She was also at his, and she was beginning to admit it, "Theo . . . you must help me escape from this prison, I hate my husband. I married him for the sake of protection, without knowing that what he wanted was just another item for his collected works of . . ." "Of art, yes, don't be afraid to say it," "Me, a work of art? Do you think so?" The rosy tips of her breasts were already grazing the young man's hirsute chest, "I will give my life, if necessary . . . my Mistress . . . But may I call you some-

thing else?" In response she placed her lips gently on Theo's. It was thus that he was no longer able to talk, but with his entire body, with his hands, his arms, his tapering pubis, he swore to her until he was breathless that he would give his life, if it was called for, to free her. (67)

In this passage the heroine, known at first as the Mistress (*Ama* in the original Spanish) and later as the Actress, achieves what appears to be a double epiphany: she formulates her hatred for her husband, who has kept her imprisoned on his island-fortress, and arouses in her servant Theo both his sexual ardor and a pledge to sacrifice his life for her freedom. On a positive, literal level, the text represents a scene of sublime emotional communion, of desire inflamed but promisingly contained, and of a small victory for innocence in its ongoing struggle against the ruthless forces of social domination (the Third Reich's military machine, her billionaire armaments-manufacturer husband, men in general). The victory proves to be short-lived, however, for each of the Mistress/Actress's saviors inevitably proves to be nothing more than the next in a line of oppressors. When she finally meets a man worthy of her trust (known only as "He" [*El*]), she is so skeptical of the masculine gender that she cannot help but suspect his motives. Her story ends with the pathetic realization, as the couple die almost simultaneously in a double hit-and-run murder, that the one who truly loved her did not survive long enough to grieve over her death.

The cited passage – and the novel's entire imaginary-symbolic register – is a good deal more complex than that profile would indicate. The Mistress is, of course, an idealized version, a rewriting of Ana, whose series of imposing men (her father, Fito, Alejandro, Pozzi) roughly coincides with the list constituted by the billionaire husband, Theo, the movie magnate, and He. Ana is not the "most beautiful woman in the world," but she is said to resemble strikingly the Austrian actress Hedy Lamarr, whose autobiography appears to have inspired roughly the first two-thirds of the sequence.[7] Like Ana, the Mistress/Actress undergoes exile, suffers from nightmares, and searches for heterosexual romantic love and freedom. An important distinction between the two stories lies in the areas in which the heroines ultimately triumph: whereas the Mistress finds amorous fulfillment (but not the freedom to enjoy it), Ana's ultimate liberation leaves her in solidarity with other women but unattached as regards the opposite sex. In this sense the two narratives complement one another, each presenting an option unavailable to the other.

The Mistress/Actress can be seen, therefore, as both being and not being the "same" as Ana. This quasi-identity, which is conveyed quite forcefully in Spanish, where only one intervocalic, nasal consonant separates *Ama* (Mistress) from Ana, is emblematic of the complexity of the problem of identities within the imaginary-symbolic narration. In a similar fashion, for instance, only one vowel distinguishes the name Theo from Thea, the name the Soviet spy adopts in order to enter the billionaire's fortress disguised as a maidservant. And in a clever play on the motif, Ana passes for her own double, for her jealous husband has placed facsimiles of his wife in various places on the island, a device that unwittingly facilitates the ingénue's escape.

The instability of personal identities extends, furthermore, to the level of the narrator who, once again, both is and is not the "same" as Ana. If the entire narrative sequence represents Ana's dreams, then it unquestionably has some strong connection with her psyche, her self. As the sharp stylistic differences between the dream passages and the diary passages underscore, however, we should be on guard against an overly facile elision of this narrator with that of Ana's waking self. If anything, this is Ana's Other's voice, that of her unconscious urges and fears, over which she has no conscious control. It is a voice Ana's conscious self might both wish to hear and be terrified of hearing.

Rather than an image of what is, this voice evokes an *imago* of what could or should be, with no necessary referent in the world beyond its discourse, except perhaps for similar artifacts of its genre. It practices, in Solotorevsky's terminology, a "rhetoric of plenitude" reminiscent of both the popular sentimental novel (the *novela rosa*, not unlike the Harlequin romances in English) and commercial Hollywood film fare.[8] Things here are satisfyingly and unbelievably self-present (although the victim of international intrigue, the Mistress is simply innocent; Theo, loving her, believes her to be so; she simultaneously falls in love with him; he pledges his life to her freedom; all these absolutely breathtaking developments coincide with his sexual arousal), as they never are in Ana's life. Within such a context, the third-person omniscient narrative point of view, with its implicit guarantee as to the "truth" within the world it represents, only adds to the oneiric quality of the writing, for truth for the waking Ana is a receding limit or horizon and not a fixed object that she can grasp at will. In a neat shift of means and ends, the kind of narration most often associated with authoritative, historical discourse is in this case redeployed to convey that which is most fantastic and unreal.

As we have seen with respect to *Heartbreak Tango*, among other Puig works, a question that arises frequently regarding playfully populist passages such as the exchange between Ama and Theo has to do with the correct construal of their meaning. Are they critically parodic of the genres they manipulate? Do they constitute a reverent homage to a more ingenuous and accessible mode of writing? Or are they nothing more than this author's idea of kitschy fun, a noncommittal stylization? Although a reasonably complete answer to these questions would be lengthy indeed (the entirety of Lucille Kerr's *Suspended Fictions* is devoted to working through these questions vis-à-vis Puig's first four novels), let me deal with them briefly by simply indicating that no single answer exhausts the possibilities of the question of correct interpretation and that, most tellingly, each answer partially veils the others. Noting – and reserving for further discussion – the pointed sign of Theo's inflamed virility, let us fade forthwith into the final passage to consider for this novel.

> [S]he got to her feet and asked, raising her voice as much as she could, where was her daughter. But no one knew what to answer her, the shooting grew more severe and the soldiers were being ordered to load up with more and more gunpowder. Suddenly a strange gust of wind arose and the nightdress was lifted, showing me to be naked, and the men trembled, and it's that they saw I was a divine creature, my pubis was like that of the angels, without down and without sex, smooth. The soldiers were paralyzed with amazement. An angel had descended to the earth. And the shooting stopped, and the enemies embraced one another and cried, giving thanks to the heavens for having sent a message of peace. . . . I heard in the distance the voice of my little girl who was telling me that she loved me very much, and that she was proud of me, and finally she appeared, and the wind lifted her little skirt and there was no doubt that she was my daughter, because she too was a pure angel. And only then did I realize why nothing was more important to me on this earth than she was, why I love her so, because she would be a woman whom no man could humiliate! because she would not be a slave to the first scoundrel who sensed that weak point between her legs, a slave to the first dog which knew to smell out her folly! (231-32)

Here we are approaching the end of several parallel pur-
suits – another imaginary heroine's quest for emancipation (a
rewriting of that of the Mistress/Actress), Ana's search for herself and
her place in the world, and the text's search for a properly attenuated concluding epiphany. After having suffered a crushing betrayal
by the man of her dreams, whom she consequently attempted to
murder, W218, the beautiful and magnanimous heroine of the
science-fiction variant of the fable, has sentenced herself to lifetime
servitude in a hospital for men with incurable contagious diseases.
Predictably, she has now fallen terminally ill herself. While in the
infirmary she meets an old woman whom everyone else scorns and
fears but whom W218 admires for her refusal to submissively accept
her fate. The tale of redemption and revelation reproduced above is
the old woman's, and her words, taken by W218 to be valid ("W218
herself had the feeling that the story was true" [233]), promise to
bring into focus the novel's diverse narrative lines as well as its title.

The slippage in narrative point of view (after the second sentence quoted above) from third to first person indicates perhaps why
W218's elderly companion is generally taken to be a raving lunatic. A
more circumspect approach, however, yields other possible senses.
The shift in narrative voice could demonstrate an exemplary drop-
ping of one's defenses – removing the mask of objectivity – in the
company of one who poses no threat. Since the old woman has a
message of import she wishes to convey, the more direct form of
address might well create an intimacy effective for establishing confidence and solidarity. In fact, an immediate bond does form between
the women, a bond whose validity is certified for the reader by the
powers of clairvoyance W218 has inherited from her unknown
mother.

On a symbolic level, to be sure, the old woman functions as the
young woman's mother (the counsel she gives transmits a vision of
freedom), and her fluid identity represents an ideal of intersubjective
relationality we have already glimpsed in, among other texts, *Kiss of
the Spider Woman*. Just as the old woman is both a "she" and an
"I," a stranger and a nurturer, W218 is both an orphan and a daughter. In fact, she is a daughter twice over, her other mother being Ana,
whose age is equivalent to the old woman's (230) and whose unconscious is the presumed source of the imaginary sequence to which
this section belongs. Focusing for a moment on the multiplicity of

Ana's identity, we see that if the Mistress/Actress is Ana's past, W218 is her future, and the crazy old woman is her other present (or present Other).

Despite the high visibility of technological contrivances (portable minicomputers for routine problem solving, "teletotal" for mass-media immersion experience, a Big Brotherly Supreme Government that effectively brainwashes and monitors its subjects), the concluding story bears strong similarities to the sentimental one told in the first half of the novel. The search for a decent and fair consort still drives the narration, the rhetoric of plenitude noted in the previous section (an unlikely coalescence of superlatives) here transformed into a utopian repression of the erotic. Rather than provide a ready complement for the lover's erect phallus (rewritten in the dream as the soldiers' firearms) or enter the fray by rejecting the ardent suitor, the solution is to render irrelevant the instrument of aggression (the shooting ceases) by blithely abandoning the space of sexuality altogether, a trait then passed on through the generations. This unsexing of woman has bewildered critics, for its truth seems to entail not so much an erasure as an absurd self-obliteration. Not only does the angelical pubis propose a literal, physical impossibility, it thrusts the onus of adaptation wholly on the gender that has already shown itself to be eminently flexible.

As the problem of freedom in the face of power is one that has concerned Puig incessantly since portraying Toto's and Mita's plights in *Betrayed by Rita Hayworth*, the passage deserves our most thoughtful consideration. First of all, symbolic victories are nothing new to Puig, for what is Valentín's concluding hallucination in *Kiss of the Spider Woman* ("This dream is short but this dream is happy") if not just such a symbolic victory? More than providing practical solutions to existential dilemmas, Puig seems to view the writer's role as finding plausible ways to emit signs that, without being Pollyannish, offer at least some reason for not capitulating to despair. Second, once we grant that the symbolic in literature may have more than just token importance, the titular formulation need not be taken as prescribing a negation of what is essentially feminine. On the contrary, it may just as well signal a move toward that which is most profoundly characteristic of woman: valor, fortitude, and generosity ("Perhaps she needs no one, her valor, her integrity, her generosity, perhaps it has already been made evident to her that the ideal man whom she longs for . . . she carries within herself" [260]).

Within a patriarchically structured culture, waiting for men to change on their own accord might take forever. Trying to force men to change – a strategy that offers no guarantees of success – would, in the short run, at the very least unleash terrible violence. To suggest that women reconceive their own worth (by not believing the prevailing myths that they are mere objects of men's desire, by finessing the either/or choices foisted upon them) and act accordingly may not be entirely fair. But, more important, such a scenario might work. In this sense, the figure of an angelical pubis can be regarded as a meritorious pragmatic answer to the thorny question of micropolitical justice.[9]

The passage cited above is certainly one of the novel's most powerful metatextual statements. A high-profile decipherment of the enigmatic title, it draws together the three narrative strands that, through generic and stylistic difference, maintain until that point their separate trajectories and identities. Once the text reaches this culminating moment, however, the differences quickly dissolve, indicating Ana's successful assimilation of the knowledge embodied in her dreams. As a result, her formerly drab existence takes on some of the felicitous attributes of the popular rhetoric of plenitude found in the two fantastic fables. Their motif of magical clairvoyance translates here as Ana's overdue realization that she is more than a man's appendage. And, almost simultaneously, she both "miraculously" overcomes her cancer and reaches out to her mother and daughter.

I would emphasize that this is not a crass capitulation to commercial interests. The seemingly facile closure of the happy ending is long since preemptively undermined and reopened. The structure of the two Hollywood-style fantasies does not coincide with the novel's symmetrically bipartite form: the Mistress/Actress's story ends before its time (part 1, chapter 7), causing W218's tale to begin prematurely (part 1, chapter 8) and spill messily into both parts. Like Ana, part 1 bears its Other within the boundaries of its self. Neither wholly "pop" nor resolutely "serious," *Pubis Angelical* systematically questions such categorical distinctions as an accurate appraisal of the Real. The prime exception to that rule remains, though, the dividing line between that which is written-to-be-erased-and-rewritten and that which is merely written.

Eternal Curse on the Reader of These Pages

In Puig's sixth novel, *Eternal Curse on the Reader of These Pages*, the erasure motif shows no sign of weakening. Indeed, whereas some key textual features are maintained at levels comparable with those of earlier texts, other aspects are treated in revised and even more highly evolved forms. In particular, by literalizing or textualizing erasure (by explicitly evoking, in the title and elsewhere, the figure of the reader and the erasures implicit in the process of reading), erasure in this novel acquires a prominence that stands without equal in the rest of the author's oeuvre.

Eternal Curse (this shorthand formulation is not just for ease of reference; after receiving numerous complaints from bookstore browsers, the Spanish publishers abbreviated the title that appears on the book's cover) focuses on a difficult relationship between two men. One is Larry John, a New Yorker trained as a historian who, in his 30s, is down on his luck, divorced, and jobless.[10] The other is Juan José Ramírez, an elderly Argentinean former political prisoner who, through the efforts of a human rights group, finds himself in New York. Larry is hired to push the ailing Ramírez, who has no memory of recent events in his life, through the streets of Manhattan in a wheelchair.

The men have at first only the most superficial of employer/ employee relationships. With time, however, they become extremely close – as close as father and son, with all the powerful emotions (jealousy, admiration, identification, pity, disdain, love) entailed in such a pairing. Then it is discovered that Ramírez kept a series of coded notebooks while he was in prison and that Larry could be the one to decipher the documents and interpret their significance. Larry could thus, in one blow, provide the key both to Ramírez's past and to his own future as a professional historian. The individual desolation of each man promises to yield to a shared well-being that springs from their mutual dependency. Whether that symbiosis can be attained and sustained is the central question addressed in *Eternal Curse*.

Like *Kiss of the Spider Woman*, this novel probes the boundaries of intersubjectivity. The objective is again the subversion of any firm distinction between *I* and *thou*, a goal of quasimystical communion between formerly estranged and suffering individuals. Instead of nar-

rating and commenting on hokey films, though, the characters in
Eternal Curse engage in "collective dreaming," a process of enacting
imagined scenes that allows them to externalize their fears and
desires, to connect with someone or something outside themselves.[11] As in *Spider Woman*, the relationship does lead to greater
self-awareness and closer human interaction for both. But in this
novel the process does not reach fruition: miscommunication, paranoia, and third-party meddling conspire to thwart the collaborative
enterprise. Potentially one and the same individual (Larry's last
name – John – and Ramírez's first name – Juan – are commonly
viewed as translational equivalents), in practice they eventually fixate
on the differences that divide them.[12]

Each feels that the other demands of him too much altruism or
self-sacrifice, and they both pull back in resentment. It is in that state
of disaffection and depression that Ramírez dies, thus making definitive the failure of their collaborative enterprise. In keeping with the
nearly absolute lack of pop-culture elements from this novel (the
major exceptions being the use of colloquial language to constitute
the ubiquitous dialogues and the blue-collar worldview to which
Larry aspires), the somber conclusion diverges markedly from the
Hollywood-style happy endings of both *Kiss of the Spider Woman*
and *Pubis Angelical*.[13] This dystopian outlook on the prospects for
satisfying human relations within a just society will characterize the
rest of Puig's fiction until his death.

In terms of narrative technique and other structural attributes,
the novel actually bears more resemblance to *Kiss of the Spider
Woman* than to *Pubis Angelical*. The action presents itself directly to
the reader through dialogue and, in the last chapter, assorted documents and letters, thus rendering the virtual narrator a transparency.
The modalities of sentimental and science-fiction writing, so
emphatically displayed in *Pubis Angelical*, are likewise absent from
this text. Their function, however, which is to represent the realm of
the unconscious and the imaginary, is preserved in a slightly attenuated form. On close inspection of their rhetorical register, some of
the "dialogues" appear not to be dialogues at all, but the product of
Ramírez's troubled psyche (they are thus disguised internal monologues, with Ramírez playing both his own and Larry's roles).[14] The
degree of scrutiny required to make such a determination and the
impossibility of reaching absolute certainty in doing so, moreover,

attest to the porosity of the frontier between fantasy and reality in this novel. The workings of the imagination are always meaningful in Puig's fiction. But in *Eternal Curse*, with endpoints blurred and distinctions problematical, their power is great; as we saw with regard to the "scientific" footnotes in *Kiss of the Spider Woman*, they enjoy near parity with the forces of cognition.

Erasure in this novel also plays an extremely important role as a theme, especially in the form of psychic repression. At the time they first meet, both Larry and Ramírez have managed to deny major aspects of their psyches, such that they are incomplete – and markedly troubled by their incompleteness. Ramírez suffers from amnesia, mostly with respect to the labor-union activities that led to his imprisonment. The loss of memory is apparently a defense against his guilt feelings for having indirectly caused the death and possible torture of his family ("You sacrificed your family for your work, you avoided dealing with your wife and children and coping with their concrete daily needs, their demands on you. And that won't let you live in peace now" [131]; "They were killed, your wife, your son and the poor French girl that raised curtains. Planting a bomb in your house was enough" [217]). But the mental block also affects his capacity to feel the most common of emotions and causes him, as in the case of a jogger in Washington Square (6), to misinterpret gestures and expressions in a way that verges on the comic. Larry, for his part, has lost his self-confidence: in spite of a salutary program of exercise and diet, he suffers from impotence with women and has dropped out of academic life, preferring instead to live in celibacy and do menial tasks that offer no challenge to his intellect.

Each protagonist, then, is in one way or another *manqué*, having effaced a significant portion of his identity. The remedy for this condition – by means of collective dreaming and other forms of complementary interaction – is to reverse the tendency toward expunction, to invert the abysmal void of life by inscribing in that void the ciphers of an integrated subject. This erasing of erasure, if you will, is no mere cancellation of the textual aspect we have been examining till now. It constitutes, rather, a second-degree, self-referential critique of the very process in which it participates. That the attempt to roll back this psychic denial does not ultimately succeed (the title promises, after all, an "eternal curse") only compounds the complexity of the picture. The utter removal or transcendence of repression (like the complete self-awareness Ana seeks in *Pubis Angelical*) emerges in the text as a receding, unreachable horizon whose unsuccessful pursuit remains as a value in itself.

The main obstacle to reaching that horizon and achieving the goals of individual wholeness and intersubjective bonding, despite the earnest efforts of all concerned, is – once again – a sort of Oedipal complex. Both characters perceive right away that their respective ages place them in a father-son relationship (Ramírez says "I'm twice your age. So you could very easily have been my son" [29]), although they do not agree on the significance of that relationship. Larry pronounces himself to be a believer in the Freudian model that characterizes him as his father's rival for the affection of his mother ("I already told you. I'm guilty of lusting after my mother, of wanting to take her away from my father, of not caring what became of him, of throwing him out in my mind, letting him wander and starve, killing him" [132]). He is thus predisposed to transfer the resentment he feels toward his father (whom he characterizes as ignorant and violent) onto figures of authority in general ("it's powerful figures that you think of doing it [i.e., vomiting] to. Not helpless creatures like yourself" [41]) and onto Ramírez in particular. At one point, in fact, they do vie for the attention of the nurse Virgo, who eventually plays a key role in the outcome of the psychodrama.

Curiously (and here Puig departs from the received model), Larry must function as a father or tutor to Ramírez, who lacks both the memory and the cultural context to understand the world in which he is thrust. In describing for Ramírez his own experiences as a youth, a lover, and a son, Larry converts himself into the authority figure against which he so desperately struggles. In such a context, if the Oedipal paradigm has application, any castration or parricide (the two outcomes available in the "classical" scenario) is sure to rebound against its perpetrator.

Ramírez's attitude toward the conflictive nature of the Oedipal theory is one of pronounced skepticism ("You couldn't miss the chance to bring in that mother business. At the least opportunity you bring it up" [207]). Despite the enormous gaps in his conscious knowledge regarding his own identity, he prefers to regard himself as a benign patriarch, replete with wisdom, generosity, and even heroism. His efforts to give Larry a raise in salary and his supportive stance vis-à-vis Larry's researching his notebooks would seem to corroborate at least some of those claims. But Ramírez can also be wrathful, abrupt, or simply incoherent, manifestations for which neither he nor anyone in the text has an explanation. His tendency to reject discussions that undermine the identity he wishes to adopt, and his outright dismissal of Larry's discoveries of his tyrannical and egocentric behavior with his family in Argentina ("I don't believe a word of it. It's all twisted, according to your whims" [216]), further bolster the thesis that his amnesia responds to a sense of guilt that is too great to confront. Despite Ramírez's repeated denials, it is clear that Larry, once his investigation was carried to completion, would supplant the older man as a figure of relative power. And the ultimate failure of their attempt to form a cohesive bond, even though it is in the interest of both to do so, lends further credence to their participating in some sort of Oedipal dynamic. Events in the text conspire, so to speak, to show the inefficacy of Ramírez's sometimes condescending, sometimes pathetic avuncular pose.

The outcome of the interaction is predictably hybrid. Rather than felicitously regaining his memory and a full sense of his personal identity, Ramírez rekindles a sensitivity to only negative feelings (resentment and a desire for revenge). Learning who he really is, it can credibly be stated, constitutes the most proximate cause of his death. Larry, for his part, appears to regain a degree of confidence in himself, but, thanks to the intervention of the less-than-pristine nurse Virgo, he loses the unique professional opportunity that would have given that confidence a channel in which to develop. We are left, therefore, with a partial parricide (a consequence of Ramírez's completed search for himself) that is also a partial castration (Larry's empowerment is at least temporarily aborted), an impure result of positing, inverting, negating, and reaffirming the Freudian paradigm. Not since *The Buenos Aires Affair* has Puig taken the Viennese patriarch of psychoanalysis so seriously, and so seriously to task.

But it is the questioning of erasure itself from which *Eternal Curse on the Reader of These Pages* acquires much of its power. This is done through the literalizing or textualizing of the matter. Heretofore, we have been reading Puig's text with an eye to the myriad forms through which the author writes by unwriting and figures through defacement. But writing itself has not constituted one of those figures of erasure. (Given Puig's penchant for either nonliterary or paraliterary artifacts, this absence comes as no surprise.) Now,

however, writing finally does represent itself undisguised. For Larry
to discover who he and Ramírez really are or can be, he must decipher the notebooks, negating everything Ramírez has said to ascertain what Ramírez has wanted to say ("to mean" in Spanish is *querer
decir* [to want to say]).

The specifics of the case are worth rehearsing. During one of
Larry's visits a package arrives from the Human Rights Committee for
Ramírez, who is suspiciously indifferent to the package – so indifferent as to suggest Larry throw it in the trash (102). Instead, Larry
opens it to find a number of novels in French, namely *Les liaisons
dangereuses* by Pierre Choderlos de Laclos (1741-1803), *La
Princesse de Clèves* by Madame de la Fayette (1634-1693), and
Adolphe by Benjamin Constant (1767-1830). Handwritten between
the lines of the texts are nonsequential numbers. By placing the
letters in the order suggested by the numbers inscribed above them,
Larry is able to decode the glyphs and fathom the message. To his
chagrin, however, the first sentence he makes out reads
"*Malédiction éternelle à qui lise ces pages*" (Eternal curse on the
reader of these pages, 102). This menacing utterance, he theorizes,
was initially aimed at any policeman who might read the notes with
hostile intent. But as things turn out, Ramírez's curse strikes none
other than Larry, the first one (along with the novel's implied reader)
to translate the exile's text.

Introduced in the final section of part 1 of the novel, Ramírez's
notebooks serve as the linchpin for every aspiration and value
embodied in the drama – Larry's flirtations with organized labor, his
hopes to climb back into a productive and satisfying role in society
and to resuscitate his flagging erotic life and self-esteem; Ramírez's
understanding of his own emotions, his personal identity, and his
pivotal role in Argentina's recent political history; the men's chance,
despite the differences in their age and cultural background, to
establish a bond between equals; and, not of least importance, the
reader's hope to discern a credible truth or truths by negotiating a
path through the maze of competing discourses. If not life and death,
deciphering the notebooks demarcates the difference between life as
meaningful experience and as vapid, merely organic subsistence. It is
in this sense that one can aver the novel constitutes a sort of
apotheosis of erasure, its enthronement and its dismantling all in
one.

In that none of these noble aspirations materializes, *Eternal Curse* marks a clear departure from the momentary, euphoric glimpses of utopia afforded in Puig's two previous novels. The torsion toward the infernal, registered in the title, stands frontally opposed to the evocations of affectionate osculation in *Kiss of the Spider Woman* and of divine innocence in *Pubis Angelical*, however layered with ironies they may be. On another plane, however, *Eternal Curse* stands in a relation of complementarity to the other two novels as regards revindicating marginalized sectors of society. All three texts, to be sure, deal with the problems of exile or estrangement, whether internal or external to one's motherland. More specifically, though, what gay males and the politically disaffected are to *Spider Woman* and women are to *Pubis Angelical*, so are the emotionally troubled, the aged, and the infirm to *Eternal Curse*. Add to that list children (most graphically portrayed in *Betrayed by Rita Hayworth*) and the simply impressionable (*Heartbreak Tango* and *The Buenos Aires Affair*), and we are very close to encompassing Puig's entire repertoire of causes. What remains is the plight of the urban poor, whose pain is shown in *Blood of Requited Love* to be so severe it literally drives one of them crazy.

Chapter Six

Tropics of Decline

Blood of Requited Love and *Tropical Night Falling*

I have just returned from the University of Oklahoma's 1991 Puterbaugh Conference in honor of Manuel Puig and am sitting with my colleagues around the departmental coffee pot. The dominant attitude seems to be one of condescending sympathy toward Puig's work in general, with disconcertion about his early demise, outright admiration for *Kiss of the Spider Woman*, and a sense of disappointment over his later novels. The most frequent substantive complaint cites a tendency to repeat earlier figures, motifs, and concerns (the womanizing soccer star, the Oedipal scenario, a defense of the disenfranchised, the engagement in lowbrow aesthetics). More impressionistic comments allude to a coasting toward entropy, a staleness, a lack of humor, and perhaps a willingness to surrender to a mood of gloom in the face overwhelming odds. Vaguely dissatisfied with these accounts (and convinced the coffee pot needs a good scrubbing with steel wool), I return to my office to ponder these questions further.

The insufficiency of these criticisms stems from two main sources. The first has to do with the assumptions implicit in making the sort of statement that alleges a lack of originality in Puig or in any other author or work. To demand that a work be absolutely original, the product of a uniquely inspired subjectivity, having nothing to do with previous cultural artifacts (either one's own or those of others), is to invoke a Romantic and now thoroughly discredited notion. We may not always know consciously where our ideas and feelings come from, but that they are derivative of preexisting texts, images, and figures that circulate in our environment there can be little doubt. Now, my colleagues are quite aware of the recycling and recombining of topoi entailed in what we commonly call creativity, so surely they are not demanding such absolute, incommunicable, and un-ecological originality. But what they are demanding is a more nuanced predominance of the new and different over the already familiar. And in so doing they are privileging rupture over continuity, as most emphatically did the surrealists in the 1920s and still do the proponents and practitioners of artistic high modernism (let us say, for the sake of brevity, those who follow in the footsteps of Proust, Joyce, Kafka, Woolf, and Faulkner). And there's the rub. For to judge an author like Puig from a modernist standpoint, when his work in many ways can be more readily associated with the cultural mode labeled postmodernism, is patently inadequate.

Few terms are as relentlessly debated among contemporary scholars and critics as "postmodernism." Without pretending to cir-cumscribe the concept categorically, what I mean in this instance by associating Puig with postmodernism is to highlight his tendency to take certain distinctions and hierarchies that modernism still cher-ishes – principal among which (as we have seen in the discussion of *Pubis Angelical*) are the dualities of "high" and "popular" culture, "male" and "female," "the self" and "the other," and "the original" and "the translation" (with the first term of each pair enjoying an unearned privilege) – and subject them to critical scrutiny. His interest in the vagaries of interpersonal relations (what I have called "micropolitics"), rather than the totalizing discourse of macropoli-tics (in Lyotard's terms, "metanarratives"[1]), is another indication of his "postmodern condition." And, especially, his bricolage method for constructing fictions, an almost random assembling of heteroge-neous cultural leftovers (images and icons multiplied ad infinitum by a profit-driven culture industry), indicates strongly that "originality," while not eschewed altogether, is far from an unassailable value in Puig's aesthetic system.

But there is more. The allegation that Puig's creative powers had begun to wane long before his death (the original publication dates of the last two novels are 1982 and 1988, respectively) strikes me as mistaken for another reason. Decline is not a vague impression one gleans from reading these texts: it is a pervasive pattern *figured in them*. Life as a descending slope, we should remember, is inscribed in Puig's novels from the outset (in *Betrayed by Rita Hayworth* Mita laments "from higher than the stars we fell" [116]). In the novels of his sixth decade, however, the vision of decline is much more deeply etched and elaborately developed. It is staged, voiced, questioned, and finally subverted, until it attains the status of a thematic and rhetorical dominant, both topic and tropics. What I propose to do in this chapter, therefore, is to examine the diverse ways in which images of downward displacement inhabit and shape *Blood of Requited Love* and *Tropical Night Falling.*[2] Rather than the exhaustion perceived by some, this investigation reveals the consummate skill with which a mature artist imparts his nuanced view of art, the self, the world, and the shifting relations among the three.

Blood of Requited Love

Josemar Ferreira, the narrator and protagonist (indeed, probably the only character) in *Blood of Requited Love*, is a builder. Trained as a stonemason and skilled as a plumber, he takes on at the age of 32 construction jobs that, of late, turn out badly. With Brazil's rampant inflation, unforeseeable delays, and unfortunate accidents, his fees often fail to cover his expenses. But things were not always so difficult, he says. Once he was young, happy, popular, and prosperous. It's only recently that things have taken a turn for the worse. That happens to the best of us, right? Well, maybe. The best of us may find ourselves on the skids now and then, but it is not clear that Josemar has ever been anywhere but where he is right now, alone and mired in poverty.[3] The former self he evokes with nostalgia – the handsome womanizer, the soccer star, the respectful son, the loving father – proves to be far and away Josemar's most ambitious construction project, a figment of his scarred imagination. The slide he describes, unhappy though it may be, serves as a symbolic shield to prevent or at least postpone the devastating collapse of his identity. The desperation of his efforts to stave off that implosion should be apparent: to save himself from sheer madness he paints a verbal portrait that attempts to salvage an uncertain past glory from a relentlessly bleak present. It is a shaky edifice at best, built as it is on a foundation of contradictory repetitions of cliché ideals. But it is all Josemar has to save him from oblivion and obliteration.

Some of the particulars of his indigency in the novel's present include the following: two-hour bus rides – when he has the fare – from his mother's home in Santísimo to Rio de Janeiro, where he works; the near certainty that the house they share will have to be sold to pay for a second operation for his mother; mounting debts resulting from his unsuccessful construction ventures; a birthday celebrated alone, with only a two-kilo pile of fried potatoes to eat and a near-empty pack of cigarettes to smoke; and two sons to whose support he cannot contribute and whose mother comes to visit to remind him of his failure. Josemar is far from indifferent to his shortcomings: much of what we read takes place during bouts of insomnia. In at least one version of his story, moreover, despite Old Testament prohibitions to the contrary, he appears to have stolen a 1,000-cruzeiro bill from an old man who wanted to regale him with a big steak. In the eyes of society and – despite his denials and evasive gambits – in his own eyes he is nothing (at times he must look in the mirror to remember his features). The anguish of his powerlessness might move some (and may yet move him) to end it all. For now, however, it provokes him to invent a past he can live with.

The focus of his illusorily perfect past, where Josemar encountered (and extracted) blood of requited love, is the seduction and subsequent insanity of Maria da Gloria. It is with her that he claims to enact the code of the ideal macho, conveyed through various samples of the bolero lyrics of the popular Brazilian singer Roberto Carlos: a firmness of word and deed, coupled with passionate longing, that is ultimately anchored in an inexhaustible sexual potency. The scene of her deflowering is one to which he repeatedly returns, as if always looking for another detail with which or another angle from which narcissistically to relish the image of himself in the act of exercising power.[4] In view of his fascination with the sex act, though, it is curious how he cannot refer to things directly, taking recourse to metaphors or euphemisms for what incarnates the unnameable (the sacred, the sublime, the nonexistent). For the male sex organ he uses bellicose but mediating terms like "saber", "staff," or "club"; the act of coitus is reduced to the neuter pronoun "that." Not satisfied with the figurative representation of his triumph, however, he feels compelled to report (or fabricate) the aftermath of his withdrawal from her body and her presence. In the case of the former, it occasions a copious flow of her virginal blood, material proof of his mastery.[5] In that of the latter, her depression and derangement, a lasting tribute to his value as an object of female desire.

But Josemar's psychic traumas run extremely deep, and even these images of triumph fail to compensate adequately. Around this primal scene he embroiders a variety of secondary figures and episodes that enrich and adorn the flattering self-portrait. These include other amorous conquests (principal among which are those of Olga, Azucena, and Valseí), automobiles and flashy clothes, and soccer performances so spectacular they lead to bedlam and conflagration. There are troubled, Oedipally charged relationships with his father and the fathers of the women Josemar repeatedly mounts, relationships he invariably manages, through charm and prowess, to convert from adversarial to comradely. His rivalries with older men stand in contrast to the rapport he enjoys with his mother, who, he reports, never tires of praising him as her most loving and accomplished son. And, finally, we have the less fortunate ones, characters like his brother Zilmar, who is small, black, and adopted, and Rogerio, a friend who died of a snakebite, in contrast to whom Josemar feels secure and superior. These elements (and more) contribute to Josemar's attempt to create for himself a paradisiacal past, thereby deferring indefinitely the impending obliteration of his disintegrating personal identity.[6]

It is not immediately obvious that Josemar's tale is unreliable, but neither is its suspect nature cloaked in impenetrable camouflage. From early on the curious dialogue that constitutes the narrative (typically, although not exclusively, a first-person query alternating with a third-person response) instills doubt as to the veracity of some of its claims ("And what did we talk about at that dance? I want to see if you're telling me the truth" [5]). These questions soon transform into direct accusations of lying ("That's not true, they wouldn't let you people into my house, I'm sure of that" [13]), allegations that prove nothing, but should put the reader on alert as to the instability of one speaker or the other (if not both). The responses to the questions also contribute to an atmosphere of doubt. In addition to the reader's likely initial difficulty in deciphering the identity of the third-person speaker, that speaker's excessive dependence on phatic (noncommunicative) formulations, such as "right?" and "is that clear?" inevitably casts suspicion as to whether indeed the claims are right and clear.

The relativity (or nullity) of truth suggested here emerges as one of the primary ideological underpinnings of Puig's polyphonic novels. In the case of *Blood of Requited Love*, however, that uncertainty does not emerge from a plurality of indeterminately authoritative perspectives. Here it is a single subject who returns obsessively to the same events, each time embellishing their telling differently and thus contradicting himself, or at least contradicting the self that described the scene previously. And so, for example, the first time Josemar mentions the deflowering he claims it occurred at a hotel in a nearby town. Later he states it happened in a thicket in the countryside, either lying on the ground or standing under a tree. A third time he places the same scene in a shed behind his mother's ranch. And a fourth version relates how, in the shed, the mother intervened so as to disrupt the planned seduction before it could transpire. Which, if any, of the stories is true is of course something beyond our power to decide.[7] What does seem certain, however, is that Josemar's insistent verbalization functions more as a shade than as a window, veiling a truth that is too painful to confront unadorned. Once we are attuned to the pattern of discordant narration, the contradictions and inconsistencies prove to be abundant.

To begin with, since everything appears to have happened in Josemar's past, the validity of his narrative depends entirely upon his memory. Fortunately, he tells us, his powers of recollection are excellent, perfect. When he fails to remember the name of a soccer teammate or that of the friend who was killed by a snake (elsewhere identified as Rogerio), however, we have reason to doubt his powers of total recall. And when he admits to forgetting the face of Maria da Gloria and on occasion even his own face, his entire enterprise is clearly in danger. Other glaring inconsistencies include the make of car he drove (was it a Maverick? a Gordini?), if indeed he ever drove a car; the number of women with whom he sired his sons (was it two, as he states at first, or one?); where he went after seducing Maria da Gloria on that Saturday night (into the arms of another woman? straight home to the farm?); and whether Zilmar visits him in the present or if that visit is just another simulacrum. There are many, many more.

What one must finally ask is whether it is Maria da Gloria who loses her mind after he leaves her or if he is not projecting his own fear of going mad onto her. The expression "to go crazy" is of course commonly used in a figurative sense, without necessarily conveying the clinical meaning of insanity. Josemar's statements to the effect that Maria da Gloria "went crazy" from his kisses or from missing him, or he "went crazy" looking at her exposed buttocks or waiting impatiently for a soccer game to begin do not by themselves indicate he is overly concerned about his own mental stability. But we should take into account the insistence with which Josemar posits as a distinguishing quality of the insane their tendency to talk to themselves ("he talked to himself like a crazy person" [39]; "After the fifteen days he said to himself, talking to himself like a crazy person" [83]). And what is this novel, after all, if not an extended dialogue between the reality principle and the pleasure principle within a single unstable individual?[8]

But even to call the interaction of voices a dialogue is to beg a question that demands sustained analysis. To begin with, there are more than two voices. First there is the self-contradictory but grammatically unified voice that narrates from a third-person, male, fair-skinned point of view (presumably that of Josemar, distanced from himself to lend historical authority to his primary worldview). In addition, there are at least five other voices: those of Maria da Gloria, Lourdes (the mother of Josemar's sons, or at least one son), Josemar's mother, Zilmar (Josemar's adopted black brother), and Josemar in the past. As stated, the basic scheme consists of a dialogue in which Maria da Gloria asks questions and Josemar answers them. Sometimes, however, Maria da Gloria's utterances are statements rather than questions ("Matías went to study and I never saw him again" [149]). Other times, when her questions or assertions strike dangerously close to the core of Josemar's deceptions, his responses appear to be irrelevant to or evasive of her indagations. Gloria: "Now I have something to ask you, why have you begun to think so much about me? For years you hardly ever did, if you did at all." Josemar: "There were eleven brothers and sisters, right?" (23). Additional variants include the substitution of another voice (Lourdes's, his mother's, Zilmar's, or that of Josemar's past) for that of Maria da Gloria, switches that can be recognized by the carping, tender, servile, or defensive tone of the particular utterance. During one period of crisis, moreover, several of these voices speak almost at once, quarreling with one another despite their representing aspects of Josemar's life that diverge in place and time (119-20).

The only plausible explanation for such an acrimonious reunion (if we felt compelled to defend the text's verisimilitude on the level of the *énonciation*) would be that these verbal exchanges represent psychic activity within Josemar, whatever referent the decentered, disintegrating signifier "Josemar" may designate. Within such a context, of course, we must be willing to admit that whatever "Maria da Gloria," "Lourdes," "Josemar's mother," and "Zilmar" may "say" depends entirely on what "Josemar" represents them as having said to himself. What look like direct quotations, therefore, are highly deceptive, for the voices are anything but unmediated. In contrast to Puig's other novels, moreover, in which the reader is invited to choose between competing discourses with regard to the truth, *Blood of Requited Love* poses a far more radical challenge. Here one must decide not only between competing discourses but also, given that all the voices collapse into one lone voice, between accepting *any* of the discourses or rejecting *all* the versions proposed.[9]

As a result, in another unforeseeable and far-reaching reversal, the most meaningful decline figured in the novel turns out to be suffered not by Josemar – who, with apologies to Richard Fariña, has been down so long he has to invent an "up" to convince himself he has any existence whatsoever[10] – but by the text's implied reader, who must contend with degrees of ontological and epistemological certainty that plummet to depths unprecedented and never replicated in Puig's oeuvre. Those record lows in the character's self-esteem and the truth value of his discourse are attained, however, through a panoply of complex and provocative narrative techniques that, while not absolutely without precedent, reveal an authorial strategy to reuse and recombine extant cultural forms in such a fashion as to put in question, as Borges and others before have done,[11] the facile distinction between innovation and renewal.

Tropical Night Falling

The last novel Manuel Puig wrote and published during his lifetime, *Tropical Night Falling*, gives an immediate clue as to how one ought initially to take the downward displacement figured prominently in its title. The opening lines consist of a dialogue between two elderly sisters, Luci and Nidia, who comment on the emotional value they attach to the everyday occurrence of nightfall. Nidia: "There's such a sad feeling about this time of day, I wonder why?" Luci: "It's the late afternoon blues, when the sky starts getting dark, Nidia" (1). Sadness and the blues, nightfall and darkness are linked symbolically, as if natural and inevitable partners. Having reached the twilight of their lives, these octogenarians must confront daily the shortness of breath, the aching joints, the moments of confusion, and the dwindling ranks of their contemporaries that are the stuff of old age. Although they are blessed with a multitude of memories, the women's accounts of the past tend to underscore a sense of loss in the present: the loss of youth and vigor; the loss of a parent, a spouse, or a daughter; and the loss of passion and romance, as well as of traditional spiritual values. To make matters worse, the Argentinean sisters find themselves in a foreign land (natives of Buenos Aires, they are in the tropical city of Rio de Janeiro), whose language and customs they understand only partially. The life they knew – once so full of promise and potential – has by now almost run its full course, leaving them with the bitter taste of unmet goals and diminishing resources. If hope for the future is conventionally figured in terms of light, nightfall provides an apt image for the waning vital forces that precede the onset of an ineluctable death.

At their advanced age, life reduces itself to something experienced directly only by others. The sisters are consigned more and more to the role of bystanders, vicarious participants who tell or hear of the passionate vicissitudes of those still able to play an active role. Luci's neighbor Silvia, an educated, independent, "modern" woman, becomes for them in this sense not only an object of fascination but also an emblem of their plight. Long since unable to pursue their own dreams, they depend on Silvia to provide them with the verbal spectacle that sustains their existence. Silvia's failed former marriage, her frustrating relationship with Ferreira, her casual sexual encounters with other men, her affection for her son – episodes whose narration occupies a major portion of the first half of the novel – take on high relief for the aging sisters and help propel them as narrators and listeners, when as actors they are barely ambulatory.

The narrative act, which tends to employ the past verbal tense, thereby locating meaning in a previous time, implicitly devalues the present. The here and now, after all, must be inherently inferior to and less interesting than the time referred to in the story, or we would not concede to diverting our attention from our own circumstance. It follows from this, of course, that were life fulfilling, there would be no need for literature. As conditions deteriorate (as exemplified in Valentín and Molina's cell in *Kiss of the Spider Woman*), conversely, narratives and other forms of artistic representation play an ever more crucial role in bolstering one's resistance to despair.[12] The solitary Silvia may yield to the temptation to attempt suicide over her humiliating failure to win Ferreira's affection (89-90), but as long as Luci and Nidia can narrate Silvia's tale of woe, they are not likely to fall prey to the same sad scenario.

One of the stories Luci tells is about the actress Vivian Leigh, who stars in *Waterloo Bridge*, a film in which Leigh plays a young woman who has everything in life and yet seems to live under a black cloud that threatens to take everything from her (32). Luci finds it remarkable that Leigh, who was at the height of her success at the time, could play such a role convincingly, as if she knew that later in real life she would lose her health and die relatively young. While this sort of reflection repeats and intensifies the motif of decline developed on the level of the two protagonists, it does run the risk of making the notion of decline seem an impression or a personal obsession of theirs. To counter that tendency, as if to ensure the objective reality of a generalized deterioration of social conditions, the text makes frequent reference to problems that go far beyond the particular concerns of the elderly interlocutors. A magazine article, for instance, makes reference to homeless beggars as the likely cause of a blaze that destroys a historically significant manor house (41). Another article on the latest trends in rock music and movies contains a preamble to the effect that only the best performers will survive in a recessionary economy (41). Other references to typical Third World problems, such as political terror (6), runaway inflation (101), foreign debt (156), wanton violence (51), conformism (43), widespread illiteracy (150), and a proliferating multinational capitalism (46, 115), contribute to the portrait of a society whose fabric is coming unraveled.

This picture of general misery serves as backdrop, in the second half of the novel, for the story of Ronaldo, the young man who, like Josemar in *Blood of Requited Love*, comes to Rio from the Northeast of Brazil to remedy his poverty and social marginalization. Unable to find employment as a construction worker, Ronaldo must take a job as a night watchman, sleeping days on a mattress in an abandoned building. When he accepts the second job of Nidia's aide and escort and later absconds with the money Nidia gave him to pay for his wife's plane fare, the problems of underdevelopment he embodies insinuate themselves in her middle-class life. Social conditions *are* worsening, the novel insistently shows: the distance between the rich and the poor is growing ever greater, and more people have less control over their own destinies than they did even a generation ago.

Recapitulating momentarily, we can easily appreciate the sense in which nightfall, evoked in the novel's title, appears to represent a state or phase of decline that is amply developed throughout the text. But to limit our reading to that sense would be to repress an important element of both the title and the text proper. The title, in the original Spanish as well as the English translation, also contains an evocation of place – the tropics – that, although not negating the thematic concerns adumbrated above, does contextualize and condition them in a very particular fashion. The sensuality, sentimentality, and glamour associated with the Brazilian tropics (North America and Argentina, located mainly within temperate zones, are similar in this case) place the entire discussion within an aesthetic framework of exoticism that is crucial to a circumspect understanding of the novel.

In this connection, I am reminded of a conversation I had in the late 1970s with a Latin American author – of a socialist-realist bent – who asked me why Puig's novels (these were, at the time, *Betrayed by Rita Hayworth*, *Heartbreak Tango*, *The Buenos Aires Affair*, and *Kiss of the Spider Woman*; but there is no reason to exclude from the set the subsequent works *Pubis Angelical*, *Eternal Curse on the Reader of These Pages*, and *Blood of Requited Love*) had such *cursis* (sappy) titles. With surprisingly little hesitation I responded that Puig's novels were largely about style, and that the styles he most enjoyed flirting with were those that appealed to the audience's feelings rather than their intellect – the romantic, corny images often produced for impressionable consumers by the culture industry. In this sense, *Tropical Night Falling* bears the same populist imprimatur we find in Puig's other seven novels. What motivates his characters and drives his plots is a headlong search for emotional fulfillment that often overlooks the unrefined nature of the ideas at stake.

Even the cerebral Silvia, a professional psychologist who is supposedly expert in the workings of the human mind, admits that her attraction to Ferreira (a middling bureaucrat whose diffidence leads her to attempt suicide) is based on nothing more substantial than a look of childlike vulnerability in his eyes (8), a trait he shares with Silvia's former husband, Avidís (88). A similar fascination with Ronaldo's gaze leads the normally pragmatic Nidia to entrust her personal security and money to the indigent and immature watchman (104-5). These are characters, let us not forget, who melt upon hearing Rubén Darío's "Sonatina" (a turn-of-the-century *modernista* poem about a lovely princess's tearful wait for her Prince Charming), believe in destiny both kind (8, 75) and cruel (33), spout trite maxims like "They can't take that away from you" (29) and "I think she must be as good as gold" (137), and fall easy prey to narrative suspense (77). As is his wont, Puig concocts a tale about average people with average intellectual defenses.

Now, while it is tempting to strike the posture of authority implicit in disclosing such manipulative devices as bathos and melodrama (thereby inscribing a figure of the Olympian critic who condescendingly straightens out the text's garbled message), an arresting respect for candor requires this reader to confess he both does and does not respond emotionally to everything he reads, a condition that may also apply to most of this reader's readers. That is, I know better than to give in to the temptation of a purely affective response, but I also recognize that that braking mechanism entails a secondary cognitive correction that is the fruit of specialized training. And every time I refrain from connecting ingenuously with some aspect of a work of fiction or a lived circumstance, as I distance myself from that initial innocent position, I am reminded of the part of me that still wants to see the world as do Nidia, Luci, and Ronaldo. From the sympathetic treatment Puig affords these characters (the repartee between the wistful sisters is particularly engaging, see 67, 70, 78, 110), it is clear that the author, too, has sought to maintain ties to an unsophisticated worldview. Which is not to say he is a naïve writer.[13] On the contrary, what he undertakes in *Tropical Night Falling* is a critical aestheticization of the notion of decline, an ambivalent evocation of its style, rhetoric, images, and motifs. The trope of decline, understood conventionally as an integral, waning phase of the trajectory of a life or text, is within the pages of the novel held in tension, both posited and concurrently subjected to critical scrutiny.

Decline as a necessary prelude to death is shaken from its moorings, first of all, in the figure of Emilsen, Nidia's daughter, who prematurely dies of cancer, and in that of Silvia, who almost takes her own life while still in her prime. Conversely, it is Luci, the younger of the two sisters, who predeceases her 83-year-old sibling. Just as youth does not guarantee robust well-being and can well meet instant death, old age need not imply senility or decrepitude. Instead of accepting decadence and eventual collapse as an inevitability, Nidia concocts a scheme in which, by taking in strangers (Ronaldo, his wife, Wilma, and his eventual lover, María José) she can maintain an independence that bewilders her entire family. And when that plan fails dreadfully (Ronaldo steals Nidia's money and runs off with María José, whom he has impregnated), Nidia still musters enough spunk to fly back to Rio in order to accept Silvia's offer of camaraderie. The round of applause with which the novel ends may be literally in appreciation of the Aerolíneas Argentinas pilot's smooth landing (163), but on another plane the ovation surely belongs to the little old lady who, in "lifting" a blanket from the aircraft, demonstrates her determination to demote decline as a governing principle of chronological advancement. That is one cliché she will not abide.

The representative contingencies elucidated here belong to a pattern of architectural complexity that inhabits the entire text. As in *Blood of Requited Love*, the basic format of two interlocutors in unmediated (i.e., no narrator intervenes) dialogue is just that: a basic format, from which many an unpredictable excursion departs. In reality, many of the dialogues consist of narrations that are encrusted in still other narrations (see, for example, the prosaic story about a ruined dress Ferreira told to Silvia, who told it to Luci, who tells it to Nidia and to the reader [17-18]), such that the structure resembles a set of Chinese boxes that fit into other boxes and suggests an endless series of discursive imbrications. Moreover, the thematic movement of the conversations, although it falls short of inciting acrimony, does not always convey sisterly harmony. The choice of topic is rather the object of micropolitical skirmishes between the speakers (see, for example, 28, 34, 52-53, 58-59, 139, 159). The scheme of dialogues, furthermore, forms the backbone of about only the first half of the text (chapters 1 through 6). From chapter 7 on, these dialogues enter into dialogue with numerous documents (assorted letters and reports, with an occasional additional dialogue [89-95, 157-62]), some of which contain other documents, such as Nidia's letter to

Luci, which reproduces Wilma's letter to Nidia, duly translated from Portuguese into Spanish (135-37). Rather than decline, the principle of eschewing schematic representation would appear to guide the text's ensemble.

Once Luci travels to Lucerne (96ff.) the novel's temporospatial configuration likewise grows quite convoluted and occasions several intertextual references. The letters serve as protracted, long-distance scriptural conversations whose poignancy intensifies once the family plots, à la Cortázar in his story "The Health of the Sick," to protect Nidia from learning of Luci's demise.[14] Nidia's letter to Luci (who never receives it) of 25 November 1987 (128-39), nothing short of an epistolary tour de force for someone in her age cohort, can be seen likewise to constitute a graphic refiguring of the Oriental maxim of "the sound of one hand clapping."[15]

Events and subjectivities are, furthermore, dynamically inter-dependent. Luci's displacement from Rio triggers an unforeseeable peripety (reversal) in Nidia's attitude toward and relationship with Silvia. From an initial stance of stern disapproval of Silvia's behavior (Nidia calls her "a daring, irresponsible hussy" [23], "sticky", [37], and "a fast operator" [52]), she comes to sympathize with Silvia's plight (69) and eventually supplants Luci as Silvia's companion and confidante (98-99). After Nidia's attempt to organize a support sys-tem of her own collapses, she gets a phone call from Silvia (157-62) that signals her replacement of Luci is complete. On returning to Rio she will assume her sister's role, embodying Luci's quixotic vitality and compassion to complement her own skeptical rationality. Having suffered a seemingly definitive defeat, she is reborn in a fuller and more integrated ("heroic") form, ascending in true Hollywood-bibli-cal fashion as she touches down in her tropical paradise.

These comments on some of the complexities of the novel's organization and characterization do not, however, exhaust the text's mysteries. There are, in addition, a number of enigmas or lacu-nae in the story that invite conjecture as they defy convincing expla-nation. It is impossible, for example, to ascertain the identity of the person or persons whose phone calls go unanswered (30, 34, 63, 84, 93-94) or to determine – if some or all of the calls had been made by Ferreira – how those calls would have deflected the course of events in the female characters' lives. Likewise, the reader is never given access to information regarding the conclusion of Ferreira's only visit to Silvia's apartment (51). Is it too sordid or too humiliating to report, or is it simply irrelevant and trivial? Moreover, one can only guess about the role of the middle-aged woman who reportedly often visits Nidia's son's house (123). And, finally (of those mysteries I have been able to detect), what do we know about Nidia's motives regarding the case of the purloined blanket (162)? Is she building hopefully for the future or yielding momentarily to arteriosclerosis?

As in lived experience, we may impose whatever patterns we need to lend coherence to a phenomenon, or we may choose to leave the matter in its raw indeterminacy. But we should recognize that the text tends subtly both to play with and eventually to discourage facile schematism. Typically for Puig, *Tropical Night Falling* evokes the simplistic through frequent allusions to generic-quality cultural objects that employ stock formulae, pleonasms, tru-isms, and platitudes. But this is only to thwart their mere replication by placing the discarded shards of the mass-mediated artifacts in a different, highly attenuated context. In short, the novel sends us mixed signals by weaving not new but altered cloth from plain, pre-viously handled flax.

Meanwhile, back at the departmental coffee pot, little has changed. Given the paucity of critical studies or even book reviews in print on Puig's most recent fiction, it seems fair to state that few have yet been able to support or contest the claims made here.[16] The fluctu-ating and heterogeneous textual process signified by the label *Puig* has in general been reduced to a simple and static icon, based largely on, first, *Betrayed by Rita Hayworth* and, later, *Kiss of the Spider Woman*. It may be some time before readers appreciate the artistry with which Puig, a man in his 50s, like Bioy Casares and Gar-cía Márquez before him, managed to project himself convincingly into an old age he could not possibly know firsthand.[17] Or before we recognize how skillfully the questions of female desire (represented here in Silvia and long a hallmark of Puig's thematic repertoire) and class struggle (another Puig mainstay, here embodied despairingly in Ronaldo and Wilma) dovetail seamlessly with the problematics of aging to round out the issue of marginalization and lend the novel noteworthy balance and sheen.

Initially an irrepressible aficionado of movies of the Golden Age of Hollywood, in *Tropical Night Falling* Manuel Puig shows explicitly, through the incorporation of such elements as answering machines, video clubs, radio taxis, and punk-rock music videos, how he has kept up with the diverse forms of electronic simulation available to us through the burgeoning technology of our postmodern times. If there is a sign of decline to which one may gesture, it is the possible lapsus in which Nidia addresses her sister by her own name (Nidia: "No puedo, Nidia, vos tenés razón" [186]; corrected in the translation to "I can't, Luci, you're right" [137]). But, on second thought, how do we know that this is the author's slip and not the octogenarian Nidia's, or a less than punctilious copy editor's at Seix Barral? And even if the error belongs to Puig, who with eight meticulously crafted novels deserves not only the benefit of the doubt but also the right to share occasionally in human error, why criticize idly when the coffee pot still needs scrubbing?

Chapter Seven

Moral Correctness Reaffirmed
Theatrical Scripts, Screenplays, Short Stories

During a major portion of the 1980s, between the publication of *Blood of Requited Love* (1982) and *Tropical Night Falling* (1988), Puig turned his attention to the elaboration of several nonnarrative texts. These include the dramas *Bajo un manto de estrellas* (*Under a Mantle of Stars*), *El beso de la mujer araña* (*Kiss of the Spider Woman*), and *El misterio del ramo de rosas* (*Mystery of the Rose Bouquet*), and the screenplays *La cara del villano* (The villain's face) and *Memoria de Tijuana* (Memories of Tijuana).[1] The shift in emphasis away from narrative is not so surprising as it may appear. Puig's first novel, by the author's own admission, began as an attempt to write a cinematographic script, and capturing the rhythms and figures of colloquial language soon became the signature of his fiction. In addition, *Kiss of the Spider Woman* and *Eternal Curse on the Reader of These Pages* consist almost entirely of unmediated dialogue, as if Puig had long since begun abandoning narrative while still working within the novel. He had already successfully realized, moreover, film adaptations of his own *Heartbreak Tango* and of the Chilean José Donoso's disquieting novel, *El lugar sin límites* (*Hell Has No Limits*).

We could say regarding his theatrical and film scripts that Puig's diffidence toward narrative authority, a mistrust that leads him to experiment with a plethora of unconventional techniques in his novels, finally moved him to stray from the narrative genre altogether, at least temporarily. Curiously, however, that move occasions an inversion in the long-standing relation between the center and the margins. One of the features that makes his novels so unique (the absence of any unifying narrative voice) is precisely the norm in a dramatic or filmic text (where telling yields almost entirely to showing). Since Puig remains concerned about the morality of wielding power in contemporary society, in these texts he finds other ways to represent that enduring problematics (principally by controlling characterization and readerly distance), redefining in a sense the space between, or beyond, good and evil.[2]

In addition to these considerations, and for the sake of completeness, this chapter concludes with a brief discussion of assorted short texts – five stories and a screenplay scenario – that have become available in English only during the past decade. In contrast to the considerable attention Puig's novels have elicited since their initial publication in the late 1960s, these texts have been largely ignored by critics and general readers alike.

Under a Mantle of Stars: A Play in Two Acts, which premiered in Rio de Janeiro in 1982, is one of the two nonnarrative texts by Puig to be translated into English to date.[3] Set in the endless plains of the Argentine pampas in the late 1940s, the drama enacts a multifrontal struggle for domination. The struggle takes place mainly between two sets of parents for control over one daughter, but it also occurs between the members of each couple and within each individual, who tries to gain mastery over the Real.[4] If this sounds heavy-handedly symbolic, it is meant to be no less. None of the characters has a proper name; all are designated by their respective stations – Master, Mistress, Daughter, Visitor, Lady Visitor, Doctor, Nurse, Maid. And in the opening stage directions we are explicitly told, "Nothing is realistic, everything stylized, including the characters' speech" (1).

Rather than a more-or-less direct (although technically complex) representation of the sentimental lives of his creations (largely the function of Puig's novels), then, we can conceive of Puig's theater – despite the virtual absence of any authorial or narratorial figure – as itself embodying a mediation, in the sense that it consciously stages a tension between and among related ideas. The "thing itself" (that which is mediated), whether truth, meaning, or some other abstraction, remains forever as a goal or a project to be pursued. This principle of endless deferment applies equally to the characters on the stage (who are trying to interpret their world) as well as to the play's spectators (who read signs in a more conventional sense). And the reader of the drama's English translation, who tries to imagine what the performance might be like in person and in the original Spanish, is at least two more removes from this receding horizon.

What stands in the way of an immediate apprehension of the world are such things as one's memory and desires, not to mention the memories and desires of others. The couple constituted by the Master and the Mistress has lived 20 years haunted by doubts. Was the Mistress having an affair with the Master's best friend (also the father of the Daughter)? Was the friend, on the fateful night of his and his wife's death in a car crash, coming to assure the Master of his friendship or to run off with the Mistress? All that remains of that ambiguous friendship is the Daughter, whom the couple has raised as their own. Uncertain what to make of her unconventional behavior, they fear she is mentally unstable, perhaps crazy. Her own insecurities, it seems, project out and condition the "objective" world. In explaining the failure of her relationship with her fiancé, Antonio, she says, "From the very start I had the feeling that something bad was going to happen. The joy he brought me was too great, and on my own I began imagining difficulties. From that point to their coming about was a short step" (8). These prophetic lines, when repeated by other characters in other contexts, become a refrain that pervades the entire dramatic space.

With the arrival of the couple of Visitors the doubts only compound themselves. When the initial couple takes their counterparts (a couple of jewel thieves who run out of gas on their way to a masquerade) to be the Daughter's biological parents, the second couple apparently, for their own gain, decide to play along with the confusion. And when the Daughter mistakes the Visitor for her fiancé, a move that leads to her seduction in full view of the other adults, all witnesses hasten to reassure her that they are hallucinatory products of her guilty conscience. Interests both collective and private (including the spectator's need to penetrate the actors' multilayered disguises in order to arrive at a singular, stable identity for each one) conspire to invert the axes of the Real and the Imagined, when they do not eradicate the distinction altogether.

Ascertaining the truth of the situation is so important because it implies not only affirming one's own sanity but also gaining control over the other participants in that situation. If the Master is right in his version of the family history, he can either have the Daughter for himself (at one point in the second act he almost runs off with her in the manner of a lover) or retain the Mistress in a state of bourgeois domestic tranquility. If the Mistress prevails, she can depart with the Visitor, whom she perceives as the man of her dreams. The Visitor, for his part, wishes in using the Daughter both to assert his independence from the Lady Visitor and to slake his thirst for carnal pleasure. The Lady Visitor, who is momentarily touched by the Daughter's sensitive vulnerability, is motivated overall by wealth and power. And the Daughter, who is helpless to defend herself against the competing forces exerted on her by the adults' diverse discourses, wants only to be loved and protected, and yet free, regardless of whether achieving that state means accompanying her biological parents, her foster parents, her fiancé, or a psychiatric nurse appointed by the State.

None of these partial and self-interested readings of reality triumphs, however. After the two Visitors are killed and the daughter is committed to a mental institution (by a Doctor and a Nurse who are played by the same actors as the departed Visitors), the original couple is left alone only long enough to savor the moment "under a mantle of stars." Despite their insistence that it's been worth all the years of yearning and deprivation, the intrusion of the outside world on the materialization of their ideal scenario seems both imminent and inevitable. Were the following statement itself not an example of a reader's "dream fulfilled," it would be fair to characterize *Under a Mantle of Stars* as averring that the ruthless pursuit of one's dreams of fulfillment, when those dreams involve exercising power over other subjects with dreams and aspirations of their own, is not a matter that is morally neutral.

In this connection *Under a Mantle of Stars* is the elaboration of a question already raised in *Kiss of the Spider Woman* (both the novel and the drama), which also ends within a character's fantasy ("This dream is short but this dream is happy"), after having suggested that one character (Valentín) may have used another (Molina) to achieve his own political ends. The violent exploitation of the powerless, whether a middle-aged homosexual male or an adolescent orphan girl, evidently continued to concern Puig through the decade of the 1980s. What is different here, however, is the unsympathetic characterization of both the Master and Mistress, who are pathetically deluded regarding the Daughter and the Visitors, when not downright ruthless in their actions. *Spider Woman* inclines toward the utopian (both parties to the dynamic process of inter-subjective communion emerge as winners of a sort) and presents the final dream as something worth sustaining as long as possible and worth the cost even after its extinction. *Under a Mantle of Stars* partakes of the somber, dystopian worldview that marks Puig's fiction starting with *Eternal Curse on the Reader of These Pages*. Despite art's inability to designate the Real (not even the representation of that impossibility achieves a plenitude of reality), one cannot avoid seeing in *Mantle* that acting autarchically or hegemonically does occasion real suffering. If the Masters are unaware of the havoc they wreak on others, then they must be awakened, even if disrupting their star-studded reverie means inscribing on oneself the figure of a wet blanket.

Much of what I have already said about odd coupling in the novel *Kiss of the Spider Woman* (see chapter 4 of this volume) pertains as well to the theatrical script of the same name. Published in 1983, in the same volume with *Under a Mantle of Stars* (but curiously not mentioned on the volume's front cover or spine), the play was first performed in 1981. It thus marks an approximate midpoint between the publication of the novel (1976) and the release of the movie (1985). Like the novel, the drama divides itself into two parts, but instead of eight chapters per part the drama contains six scenes in its first act and three scenes in its second act: quantitatively, at least, it is front heavy. Regardless of this formal asymmetry, however, its relation to the novel is fundamentally that of a reduction: it bears many of the same features of the original (large chunks of dialogue are reproduced verbatim in the stage production) but almost always on a diminished scale.

Whereas the novel takes place primarily in a prison cell, with a few spatial jumps to the Warden's office or to Molina's apartment, the play remains exclusively within the cell. Instead of the five films Molina narrates in the novel, the play has him recount only one, *Cat People*, and precious little of that. The repeated acts of homosexual love alluded to in the novel likewise are distilled down to one love scene on stage. And most noticeable to the reader familiar with both versions is the absence in the script of the erudite footnotes on research into homosexuality. In this regard, the play is merely dialectical (responsively plurivocal, but all on the same discursive plane), whereas the novel is more truly dialogic, in the profoundly hetero-glot and polyphonic sense Bakhtin has lent that term.

Not all the author-cum-playwright's revisions cut in the same direction, however. Several aspects of the play actually show an increment in intensity or frequency over the novel. Such is the case with the use of humor, which although it tends toward the dark side (e.g., Valentín: "Today the plaster-style porridge isn't too bad" [90]), does give the script a slightly broader range of moods or modes. Similarly, Valentín in the play is outwardly more nervous or even hys-terical (see p. 114) than his novelistic counterpart.

Because of the highly visual nature of theater, one is aware, too, of the greater fluctuations in light and dark necessary to orient the viewer. Shutting the lights off suddenly in one context can mean cur-few, the end of another endless day. A change of lighting between scenes can mean the passing of a long interval of time. Other times the various shades of light can insinuate a character's mood or sug-gest a new stage in the evolution of the ongoing relationship. Whereas the blank spaces in much contemporary narrative are gen-erally considered to be potentially liberating of the reader's imagina-tion, we observe here a curious inversion.[5] Since the novel says nothing regarding questions of lighting, it is quite possible that such considerations never enter at all into the reading.

The addition that most affected this reader, however, is the clever use of a voice-over technique to indicate what happens while a character has gone offstage. Of the four such instances, three occur when Molina visits the Warden to conspire, first against Valen-tín and later, when Molina falls in love with Valentín, against the Warden and against time itself. These scenes take place while Valen-tín sits practically motionless in the cell, thus creating a pronounced disjunction between the visual and linguistic signs simultaneously broadcast to the spectator. The result of this disparity is to empha-size Molina's disingenuousness, to magnify his spidery guile: the technique alters the definition of his character. In the final scene, however, the voice-over serves a decidedly narrative function. Here Molina informs the somnolent Valentín what has transpired since Molina's departure from prison, explaining his possible motives for contacting Valentín's comrades-in-arms and rapidly bringing the play to its dénouement. The theatrical Molina comes across as less morally pure and more rhetorically effective than the novelistic

Molina – a slyer and more convincing narrator. Does this empowerment detract from his status as a heroine?

The dynamic enacted between Valentín and Molina (a relation that is adversarial and hierarchical at the start and eventually becomes collaborative and egalitarian) appears anew in *Mystery of the Rose Bouquet*, which premiered in London in 1987 and in Los Angeles in 1989 and was published in English translation in 1988. But the utopian agenda that underlies *Kiss of the Spider Woman* is here strengthened, for the characters, situated in a hospital rather than a jail, are free to continue their admirable project beyond the four walls that at present confine them. It is not a case of having to choose between bliss within the privileged space and suffering without. All the Patient and the Nurse must learn to do is to act with sincerity and to trust that the other will do the same in order to become, in the words of Elías Miguel Muñoz, "playful accomplices in a life-affirming game."[6] This solution may strike some as facile and patently unbelievable (the painful choices that confront Molina and Valentín seem more plausible according to contemporary standards), but the fact remains that *Mystery of the Rose Bouquet* stands as Puig's most unabashedly affirmative paradigm for a just social order, his most unequivocal statement of faith in humankind's capacity to progress toward a more humane state. For Puig, narrative remains the space of analysis and verisimilitude; theater and film are for synthesis and allegory.[7]

Although I find quite useful Muñoz's suggestion that we read *Mystery* through the prism of *Spider Woman* (thus accepting the formerly subservient Nurse to be a wiser and healthier Molina), there is a point at which insisting upon the analogy ceases to be productive. One would do well to be mindful of the relation between *Mystery* and *Tropical Night Falling*, for instance, where the motifs of aging and death receive a most elaborate treatment. And along with death we find the question of religion, or more precisely faith in a divinity, addressed both directly and extendedly. The characters in *Tropical Night Falling*, despite their advanced age, express their doubts about and eventually their lack of faith in God. For the Patient in *Mystery*, who suffers a prolonged depression after her only grandson dies in an automobile collision, God "got it wrong" when he created the world. Later, when the collaborative search for the truth has successfully run its course, the two ponder whether it wasn't God who finally "got it right" for a change. In a most telling exchange, the Patient says through tears of joy, "I think that today . . . the devil had a hand in it," to which the Nurse responds, "No, let's just say it was the porter [who found barbiturates in the Nurse's handbag, thus saving her from committing suicide] who helped" (50). God? The devil? The porter? The very least one can conclude is that in this inquiry the notion of a divinity, placed in competition with not only its lower-case adversary but also a humble agent at a health-care institution, is in this idealized world severely trivialized.

In *Eternal Curse on the Reader of These Pages* many of the same concerns (aging and illness considered within a psychoanalytical context) arise. One important distinction, however, resides in the outcome of the search for truth via the unconscious: all the play acting, collective dreaming, hallucinating, and delving into childhood memories in *Eternal Curse* lead to a conclusion that could be called tragic (removing the aristocratic connotations from that dramatic term). Yet in *Mystery* we read in the closing stage directions: "They both laugh contentedly" (51). Why does one pair of subjects succeed when the other fails so abysmally?

Despite the many variables at play (and therefore the difficulty of isolating a single factor), one clear distinction does lie in the characters' gender. Ramírez and Larry struggle constantly with powerful Oedipal (castrating father/parricidal son) forces, whereas the Patient and Nurse enjoy a relationship free of all traces of testosterone. Not only are they less savagely aggressive than their male counterparts, but they lack a common object of desire over which they might contend (in the Freudian scenario, the mother-lover). In fact, given Puig's overriding concern with questions of sexuality, the absence of erotic imagery of any sort constitutes perhaps this text's most salient feature (it is without precedent in the author's oeuvre). What works for the goose may not work for the gander, but in this case omitting the gander comes close to eliminating gender altogether.

The pivotal role Puig assigns to sexuality in redeeming mankind suggests another text we might use to help understand this *Mystery*, and that is *Pubis Angelical*. In that novel Puig posits a solution for the problem of women's exploitation: asexuality. The angelical pubis, the unsexed sex, offers the prospect of eliminating libidinal desire from human interaction and, by extension, freeing the entire species from the irrational forces that govern our behavior. Similarly, in their effort to arrive at the truth (as to their personal identity, their pain, their need for camaraderie), the Patient and the Nurse in *Mystery* manage to eschew all matters of a prurient nature, freeing themselves of the need to play deceitful power games. The key to society's basic ills, according to Puig, lies both within the human psyche and on the human anatomy. In that we cannot in reality divorce ourselves from our sexuality, however, this conceit serves also as an index of the unbridgeable gap between our history and our aspirations.

The characters' willingness to share authority extends even to the play's title. *Mystery of the Rose Bouquet* does not belong to the mystery genre, in which detectives typically solve problems of a criminal nature; its only investigative work involves, for the characters, delving into the human unconscious and, for the reader-spectator, as usual, interpreting signs. But a question does arise regarding one of the Nurse's fantasies in which she finds herself in a garden with a bearded gentleman and a rose bouquet (31). This image, which remains inconclusive and enigmatic as to the gentleman's fate and the source of the flowers, reappears several times throughout the play and is picked up finally by the Patient, who states, Garbo-like, "I want to be alone to remember the many times I received a rose bouquet" (51).

According to Muñoz, the floral figure symbolizes "completion, consummate achievement, the beloved's heart" (252), and it is tempting to accept that commonsense reading. Yet nowhere in the text does anyone or anything attempt to decipher its value, to limit its range of meaning: despite their mutual suspicion and class differences, among others, the characters wisely refrain from treading on the sacred ground of one another's epiphanic reveries. According to Umberto Eco, "the rose is a symbolic figure so rich in meanings that by now it hardly has any meaning left: Dante's mystic rose, and go lovely rose, the War of the Roses, rose thou art sick, too many rings around Rosie, a rose by any other name, a rose is a rose is a rose, the Rosicrucians . . . . A title must muddle the reader's ideas, not regiment them."[8] While we continue to ponder the characters' formula for success in *The Mystery of the Rose Bouquet*, we should not overlook the sublime respect implicit in their reciprocal silence regarding the text's master trope. As many professional critics and teachers can attest, interpretive authority is an extremely difficult sort of authority to share, and achieving that delicate state of restraint may be the ultimate test of human perfectibility.

The Villain's Face (*La cara del villano*), a film script adapted from "The Impostor" ("El impostor"), a story by the Argentinean author Silvina Ocampo, is a gothic tale with a curiously didactic bent. As it intrigues or repulses the viewer-reader with its disconcerting and horrific images, it also demonstrates why one ought to avoid interpretive hubris (pride). An allegory of misreading, the script first lulls spectators into a false sense of security regarding their interpretive authority and then violently dispels that complacency, thus instilling in them a secondary, corrective mechanism against cocksure judgments.

From the outset, all signs point toward a straightforward understanding. A sketch portraying a tiger and a lamb, displayed in the film's initial sequence, seems to indicate a clear-cut case of victimization. Armando Heredia, a reclusive young man, is acting so strangely that his father sends his lifelong friend, Tabares, to ascertain the exact nature of Armando's problems. After a trip that includes the strange disappearance of a lovely young lady and a taxi driver's unexplainable reluctance to approach the Heredia hacienda, Tabares arrives to discover the place dreadfully neglected and occupied by eccentric and menacing characters. He learns that Armando has suffered some sort of "accident" and finds a diary supposedly written over the past few days by Armando's friend Luis. Tabares's reading of the diary takes the form of a flashback that constitutes a major portion of the film.

In the diary Luis describes his journey, strongly analogous to Tabares's, to visit Armando as Luis had done five years before. Despite his attempt at rekindling the friendship they shared on the previous visit, Armando's lies and inconsistent behavior produce in Luis only distrust. The presence of a grotesque monster, El Negro (Blackie), rumored to have been blinded by Armando, and several other contradictions and repetitions add to the atmosphere of dread. It soon becomes apparent that both young men are in love with the same young woman (known to Luis as Claudia and to Armando as María). When Armando has Luis pose as the lamb for a series of sketches he is drawing, it is difficult to resist surmising that in the inevitable confrontation between the rivals, Luis will be defeated if not destroyed. The villain's face in the sketch clearly belongs to Armando.

Or so it seems. When Tabares finishes reading Luis's diary he is astonished to learn that Armando has had no visitors over the past week, that he has, rather, been obsessively writing in the very diary Tabares (along with the viewer) was reading. The villain's face associated with Armando is, first, Armando's creation. In addition, that face is the projection of the proxy-father, Tabares (who as a retrospective clue to his confusion gives Claudia-María the same face as the lovely young lady he met on the train). The "real" Luis, who attends Armando's funeral service (the "accident" was fatal and self-inflicted), is utterly different from the victim Tabares imagined. In fact, as we see in the final scene, he is the opposite: an executioner who shows no remorse at having caused the attempted suicide of the "real" María, whom he again possesses, and the successful suicide of his friend Armando. In the concluding sequence a corrected version of Armando's sketch appears, with the faces reversed: Luis's visage occupies the place of the villain.

The peripety achieved by this screenplay is immensely effective. It does not victimize inattentive viewers (who, after all, are innocent lambs) but rather traps lucid viewers in their own plotting snares. The text lays down a series of false clues that, promising a coherent if pat solution, depends for its impact on the viewer's effortful investment in the wrong answer. That sleuthing scenario, moreover, figures in the context of a generalized play of appearance and reality in which truisms are used to create false expectations – expectations that are later exploded. There is the cliché, for instance, that films are structurally simple, especially as compared with narrative. In this case, however, with flashbacks within flashbacks, the indeterminacy of the three main characters' personal identities, and the radical revision of the meaning of key events, we find a structure of Byzantine complexity. Another stereotype would have youth as a time of innocence and idealism, an association encouraged by the characters' principal means of transportation, the bicycle. But the aspects of youth emphasized in this instance are its unbridled lust, its perverse duplicity, and its anxious doubts and apprehensions. Blackie's scarred and blinded eyes, which at first suggest Luis's successful taming of the concupiscent beast within, really reflect our own eyes, which fail to see their own blindness.

Within this context, even the final, corrected version of Armando's sketch must be taken as provisional, an appearance whose interpretation is subject to possible future revision. After being shown the wages of hubristic confidence in our interpretive authority, we should be wary of accepting our own facile judgments, even when validated by the likes of proxy-fathers like Manuel Puig or Jonathan Tittler. Perhaps the most troubling conclusion to which *The Villain's Face* leads us is the prospect that our most cherished convictions are not at all our own. They are the product of projections imposed on us by countless, faceless others.

Puig's other published screenplay, *Recuerdo de Tijuana* (Memories of Tijuana), appears in the same tome as *The Villain's Face* but, as if handled by an indolent agent, receives a decidedly second billing. Not only is its title mentioned last, it is not represented in the front-cover sketch (a rendering of two faceless young men with a black dog in front of a tree in whose trunk is etched the name "María," an obvious allusion to *The Villain's Face*). Moreover, in the author's prologue, the film script merits only one perfunctory paragraph of commentary ("As for the second script that completes this volume, *Memories of Tijuana,* it was also ordered by Manuel Barbachano Ponce in 1978. It was never filmed, although from time to time the possibility of carrying out that project is mentioned" [14]). Yet, unlike its companion piece, *Memories* is not an adaptation of another text but an original composition. Its treatment of ethical questions, whether implicit in the act of interpretation or in human behavior in general, is no less imposing, moreover.

What may explain the text's subordinate status, other than the author's modesty, is its vulgar veneer. Whereas *The Villain's Face* situates itself within the generic space of the gothic horror tale (an originally literary phenomenon), *Memories* evokes nothing so much as thousands of Mexican cabaret movies of the 1940s and 1950s, featuring stars such as Dolores del Río and Jorge Negrete, against a backdrop of *rancheras* and *boleros*, and exploiting predictable intrigue, manipulative sentimentality, and titillating spectacle. As such, the script belongs to the margins of an already marginal literary genre, the screenplay. In keeping with Puig's penchant for parody (in the sense of recontextualization of prior texts and textual models), however, the text's cardboard schematism leads to a startling peripety whereby it switches codes and reinterprets its own conceptual framework. Melodrama metamorphoses into metafiction as straitlaced morality yields to a higher authority: a gut-level sense of fairness and solidarity with common folk who struggle to survive without the benefit of, and often in opposition to, powerful social institutions. While this assessment may enable us to appreciate some of the text's veiled subtlety, it leaves unanswered the question of its lowly placement within Puig's oeuvre.

Banality, although a pretext for a later self-critique, permeates the film at every level, including its hackneyed plot, its base use of language, humor, and sensuality, its stereotypical characters, and its rudimentary narrative technique. The film's present action consists mainly of sequences in which a young man named Fernando drives from his home town near Hermosillo (in the northern Mexican state of Sonora) toward Tijuana, on the U.S. border. As he flees from threatening underworld figures, he recalls the events leading up to his present predicament. In Tijuana he hopes to find La Carnada (literally "bait" – from *carne*, which means "meat" or "flesh" – but also in a figurative sense "trap" or "artifice"), a dance-hall singer with whom he worked before. After she killed their boss, they fled to Tijuana on a voyage parallel to the one currently in progress (La Carnada also relates parts of the plot through her own recollections while in jail). When he reaches his destination, however, he learns she has been released from jail and is now the moll of another hated gangster, El Moreno ("The Brown Man" or "The Swarthy One"). He solemnly rejects her declarations of love and her plea that they run off together. Tired of her life of masochistic degradation, she kills her master-lover El Moreno, whose henchmen in turn kill her. Bewildered and incredulous, Fernando can only retreat from the scene.

Within this diegetic framework, the major portion of the action (related in flashbacks) consists of stock bits such as a farewell scene between the fugitive hero and his stolid *campesina* mother; a kidnapped, drug-addicted *gringa* named Laurie, the daughter of the big boss of the drug ring who lives across the border in Los Angeles; several crowd scenes in night clubs and a cockfight arena; a rape before the eyes of a suffering father; three assassinations and numerous beatings; and liberal doses of moralistic pontificating by the protagonist, Fernando. Much of the dialogue is in one form of slang or another (first that of university students, then that of the underworld into which Fernando descends), and several sequences entail cheap linguistic gags (confusion between *chino* and *chingo*, Laurie's tortured Spanish syntax) that seem designed to keep viewers from growing bored while the plot gradually takes shape.

Even the most developed characters (Fernando, La Carnada, and Sobredosis) lack a modicum of psychological depth. As indicated, Fernando tends to speak in pious platitudes. Before definitively breaking with his college sweetheart, he says, "The time spent with those sick people made me want more and more a peaceful life, at Laura's side" (99); when La Carnada informs him of the depth of her feeling for him he responds, "I'm going to help you because you saved my life. But that's where it stops, because I'm of a different class, better or worse, who knows . . . but of a different class. And I don't like to mix things up" (112); to the very end, even with blood-thirsty goons on his heels, he protests, "I didn't do anything wrong" (144). At times Fernando's innocence (in the sense of naïveté) verges on the diabolical.

More interesting than this unidimensional self-righteousness is the assortment of disparate stereotypes that constitutes La Carnada. On the one hand, she is a floozy who drinks, smokes, and, until meeting Fernando, makes herself available to the guy with the fattest wallet. On the other hand, she has talent: she improvises a stand-up comic routine that saves Fernando's job by leaving the cabaret audience howling in the aisles. She is also linguistically gifted: she can translate between English and Spanish, serving the power broker El Toques (The Toucher/Toker), much as La Malinche did Cortés in his conquest of New Spain. Her masochistic relationship with men, while reminiscent of Gladys in *The Buenos Aires Affair* and Molina in *Kiss of the Spider Woman*, finds a plausible (if reductive) explanation in her being raped before her father's eyes in her adolescence. And, most saliently (with apologies to Tammy Wynette), she "stands by her man" (until she finds another one).

This leading lady of the night is complemented by Sobredosis (Overdose), a corpulent, man-hungry, street-smart informant who, despite her loyalty to a rival gang (she works for the Hermosillo group that conspires against the band from Tijuana), respects La Carnada's ability and sympathizes with her problems regarding the opposite sex. Significantly, it is Sobredosis who has the last adjudicating word, after La Carnada dies and Fernando continues to insist on his innocence. Her line, "I like people who are crazy like her [La

Carnada] . . . The sane ones like you . . . make jailers" (146), contains the seed of a subversive rereading necessary to appreciate the depth of all the schlock we have been describing.

The shift away from a simple, monologic tale takes place gradually and does not culminate until Fernando comes to a belated realization (the technical, Greek-derived term is *anagnorisis*) in the form of a comeuppance from La Carnada. At that point she explains the meaning of their relationship from her perspective: "I went to Hermosillo under orders from El Moreno. In order to see if I could find a gringa who had gotten lost. And I found her. And later you gave me an excuse to wipe out El Toques, a favor I did for humanity" (138). Until that moment the bifocalized narrative (Fernando alternates voice-over remembrances with La Carnada as he flees and she waits in jail) seems insignificant because merely formal: they appear to tell the same story. But once deep dialogism is established (through the independence of her voice, which relativizes Fernando's narrative authority), there is no returning to discursive ingenuousness. And just to be sure, a third reading, that of Sobredosis, is introduced: "Didn't you ever hear of professional stool pigeons? Well, I'm one. I've been following the two of you since the beginning. . . . I sell information, like others sell tamales, or morphine. The only thing that matters to me is that my two kids are studying in Mexico City and they don't lack for anything. One is already in the University" (139-40). Gang warfare and a mother's overriding concern for her children's welfare are two mitigating factors that never enter Fernando's mind. His stubborn adherence to an inappropriately rigid moral code replicates the unifocal viewer's insistence on a straightforward, genre-bound interpretation of the text (a monstrous, Cyclops reading). As with *The Villain's Face*, this screenplay teaches spectators hermeneutic humility.

Consider for a moment the script's use of language, which is so thick with lower-class Mexican jargon as to make a literal reading difficult for a nonnative. Even though Puig resided in Mexico for two extended periods of his life, this is not his own slang, which would be more akin to the domestic chatter one finds in the opening chapter of *Betrayed by Rita Hayworth*. The linguistic register of *Memories of Tijuana* (replete with *ándale, pinche, chingada*, and other lower-class Mexicanisms) is a stylized exaggeration of the idiom (in the broad sense, including sets, gestures, music, and mustaches, either pencil thin or bushy à la Pancho Villa) of grade B Mexican film, itself an exaggeration of street argot. It is an idiom Puig was thoroughly familiar with, and both loved and deplored. The point is, however, that the language does much more (and much less) than build character portraits and advance the plot. It evokes a world of artifice and technique, of commodified images that have circulated widely and now fold back upon themselves to reveal their constraining, codified nature and, when recontextualized, their continued capacity to generate meaning.

As usual with Puig, it is easier to formulate what moral correctness in *Memories of Tijuana* is *not* than what it is. Fernando's blind faith in a bourgeois ethic of stable domesticity and upward mobility is surely inadequate for large sectors of society, which lack access to the basic necessities of shelter, food, and clothing, much less adequate health care or education for advancement. The Judeo-Christian tradition at the source of that bourgeois ethic has come under severe attack within the past generation for implicitly and unfairly favoring heterosexual males and people of fair complexions. But once we defy mainstream doctrines and even exceed the bounds of legality, where do we draw the line? One possibility would be total anarchy or libertarianism, where no laws or behavioral codes infringe upon individual freedom. A reasonably close look at any of Puig's texts reveals he does not espouse this sort of free-for-all. Another option, which he also rejects, would be armed insurrection leading to a wholesale overturning of the status quo (eliminating class differences, along with those pertaining to age, sex, race, religion, and the like) – the sort of revolution embodied in a figure like *Spider Woman*'s Valentín. So-called wars of liberation in Latin America, from Madero's Mexico to Castro's Cuba, have established a poor track record over the years for respecting the human rights they claim to champion. Despite rhetoric to the contrary, authority merely changes hands while abuses of power against marginalized groups continue unabated.

Again the solution, if there is one, lies on a more modest, micropolitical scale. When La Carnada saves Fernando's job (he is a flop as a crooner and she rescues his act by injecting a comic counterpoint), she expects and convinces him to help her escape from Hermosillo. So far, so good. But when at the end she declares her love for him and asks him to flee from Tijuana with her, despite his affection for her (which, even after sleeping with her, he condescendingly dismisses as pity) he rejects her, essentially killing her. He cannot accept her as an equal, for that would imply abandoning the effete, hierarchical system of his upbringing. The alternative to the monolithic ethical doctrines articulated in *Memories of Tijuana* consists of an ad hoc intersubjective justice that embraces loyalty, mutual respect, and kindness reciprocated. It is a piecemeal solution, as are all real (read "historical") solutions to real problems. Puig's tendency to grant privilege to the concrete and contingent over the abstract and eternal (along with his refusal to entertain a sharp distinction between mass culture and high culture) explains why many critics, despite the author's fascination with issues of morality, associate this contemporary author with literary postmodernism.

To conclude this discussion of Puig's nonnovelistic works, we turn to several stories and an unfinished film script recently published in diverse journals and anthologies in the United States. In chronological order they are three vignettes of homosexual life in New York, "The Black Detective," "The Sado-Masoch Blues," and "Classical Farah," which figure in an anthology of Latin American gay fiction, *My Deep Dark Pain Is Love* (1983)[9]; "The Usual Suspects," a dialogued story that appeared in the journal *Review* (1991)[10]; "Vivaldi: A Screenplay," the truncated draft of a script Puig was working on when he died, published in the *Review of Contemporary Fiction* (1991)[11]; and "Relative Humidity 95%," an avant-garde story included in the anthology *A Hammock Beneath the Mangoes* (1991).[12]

The trilogy of vignettes, none of which exceeds two pages in length, bears a single theme in common: the sordid turn life has taken for gays in New York. They also share a common narrative technique, a first-person monologue (or monologues encrusted in other monologues) that manages to portray the speaker without overt external intervention. In "The Black Detective" an author-figure resembling Puig himself frames the narration of a "hotel queen," an elegant gay who speaks of himself as a woman and delights in picking up straight men in the corridors of luxury hotels. "The Sado-Masoch Blues," set outside New York's kinkiest sado-masochist bar, where the author-figure records the speaker's words, consists of the rambling, cynical monologue of an aggressive, guilt-ridden devoté of self-degradation. The voice in "Classical Farrah," that of a Jewish

Venezuelan gay who would rather associate with heterosexual men
than "girls" like himself, laments the transvestitism, lesbianism, and
other "extreme" forms gay life has taken in New York (presumably in
the 1960s, when many puritanical cultural constraints evaporated).

From these minimal samples, one easily imagines the flamboyant
gestures and costumes that accompany the voices. All three demonstrate Puig's capacity for capturing an entire existence and its cosmos
through the cadences of spoken language. In addition to the skillful
manipulation of the outrageous narrative voices, the sketches are
highly noteworthy for their exclusive focus on a thematics of homosexuality, something which Puig has in general avoided. At almost a
decade's remove from their publication (and perhaps two decades
from their composition), too, the pieces seem almost tender, despite
their transgressive subject matter. As with *Spider Woman*, not a
word refers to the scourge of AIDS.

"The Usual Suspects" represents several stories Puig wrote
directly in Italian in 1989 and 1990 and published in the magazine
Chorus. It stages, without the mediation of a narrator, a long-distance phone conversation between Anna, the chair of a program in
Italian culture at a U.S. college, and Carlo, a film historian living in
Italy. Anna's purpose in calling is to have Carlo send her some video-
cassettes of films made during the fascist period between the two
world wars. She contends that leftist film critics, who rallied around
neorealism in the aftermath of World War II, confused aesthetics
with politics by censoring such masterpieces as Camerini's *Men:
What Scoundrels!* and *Mister Max*. This is vintage Puig: the woman
prevails, ideology falls before artistic considerations, film erudition
parades itself in plain raiments, and no narrator intervenes to send
the wrong signals to the powers that be.

"Vivaldi: A Screenplay" is a truncated hand-written draft, in the
author's own English, of what might have become a movie script if
Puig, still in his 50s, had not died. It consists of four scenes or
sequences, most likely from the beginning of a story about the life of
the brilliant but sickly baroque composer Antonio Vivaldi. Set in
Venice in the early eighteenth century, the script first depicts a conversation between an impresario and a soprano who have learned
that, because of health problems, Vivaldi will not compose the opera
they have requested of him. Undaunted, they go in search of Vivaldi,
first to the parish where he ministered, then to his parent's home,

and finally to a convent in the countryside. Each step of the way adds to the impression that the composer is an eccentric genius, irascible and impervious to propriety. In the last sequence the searchers hear emerging from a distant stable the strains of beautiful violin music, presumably that of Vivaldi. And there the fragment stops. This is a very rough first sketch, replete with cross-outs, lacunae (Puig could not remember the word for "skein" [*madeja*]), and questionable semantic usages. It does permit, however, a rare glimpse into an early stage of the creative process. Puig's choice of English is not without precedent: *Eternal Curse* was first recorded and transcribed in English. But as a screenplay, "Vivaldi" appears designed to be sold to a Hollywood studio, perhaps along the lines of the 1985 success *Amadeus*.[13]

Of this heterogeneous array of texts, the most substantial by far is "Relative Humidity 95%," which in a technically complex manner conveys the situation of a modest Argentine family on a summer morning in Buenos Aires. Although they share the same house, the three characters – a man, a woman, and the man's son (the woman is the boy's stepmother) – live in separate worlds. The husband suffers from a cold, the heat, the effects of nicotine and caffeine, and the vagaries of running a small business in Argentina's uncertain economic and political climate. The woman lives attuned to history, to nature, and the interconnected organicity of life: she tends to console or accommodate the man. The boy awakes after an anxious night of studying for an exam and of masturbating. Each character's impressions and perceptions are intermingled with dialogue, newspaper excerpts, and some narratorial mediation. The man wants to deny knowledge of the boy's nocturnal activities, while the woman insists they should "tie [the boy's] hands when he goes to bed at night" (77). The story ends with no evident closure, suggesting rather a continuation of the discomfort, inner turbulence, and tenuous communication depicted in this disquieting family portrait.

The diversity of contemporary urban life makes discussing morality increasingly difficult, if not impossible. Yet, as we have seen, Manuel Puig manages not only to raise moral issues but also to do so in a nuanced and refined form. Simplifying for the sake of gaining a summary overview, note that in *Under a Mantle of Stars* he demonstrates some of the tragic consequences of acting autarchically in the pursuit of one's dreams. *Kiss of the Spider Woman*, while maintaining the innocence of mutually consenting sexual activity and the fea-siblility of mitigating radical differences among individuals, suggests in its theatrical version the question of the empathetic limits of empowerment. The closest thing to a full-fledged morality play one is likely to find nowadays, *Mystery of the Rose Bouquet* proposes old-fashioned altruism as a prime ingredient for enacting social justice and for overcoming existential estrangement. *The Villain's Face*, as it spins a snarled tale of diabolical tyranny, offers a critique of interpre-tive authority designed to chasten the most self-sufficient reader. And *Memories of Tijuana*, while continuing the play of deceptive appearances found in *The Villain's Face*, redefines righteousness in the light of social contingencies.

As for the uncollected texts described above, the ostensibly gay pieces make no moral judgment regarding the characters portrayed therein, but, as with *Kiss of the Spider Woman* (see chapter 4), there is an implicit stance taken by merely portraying so graphically the at-times Felliniesque countenance of homosexuality. "The Usual Sus-pects" enacts a David-and-Goliath scenario (both as to the woman film scholar and the directors whose films she defends), an archetype at the root of Puig's whole enterprise. The Vivaldi frag-ment is too truncated to allow for a responsible assessment (itself an ethically driven statement), but it is interesting to observe that for Puig, practically to his dying day, the "language of film" continued to be English. And "Relative Humidity 95%," in open-ended fashion, asks about adolescent masturbation whether denying its existence or prohibiting its practice are not the only choices imaginable.

Synthesizing even farther, we see how Puig, like his compatriot Julio Cortázar, treats the specialized matters of reading and writing on a continuum with questions of general concern, such as death, sex, power, and mass culture. Ideology frequently works to the detriment of aesthetics, as readers like Juan Goytisolo use Cortázar's *A Manual for Manuel* (1973) to illustrate.[14] It is to Manuel Puig's enduring credit that he was able repeatedly to strike a balance between those polar forces (that, in brief, is the drama staged in *Kiss of the Spider Woman*). The key would appear to reside in Puig's exemplary forbearance and tolerance, his rare capacity to represent through his fictions questions (moral and otherwise) pertinent to existence in the second half of the twentieth century, without steer-ing his readers and viewers to a monolithic, preconceived answer.

Chapter Eight

Re-viewing Puig

Puig's dialogical fictions, rich in montage-like performativity and nonliterary language, resist summary recapitulation. Still, there is much to be gained by rehearsing the salient aspects of his texts, for certain insights appear only at a synoptic level of generality. The filmic/video medium suggested in the subtitle above alludes not only to the visual aspect of his prose (which, alongside the aural/oral dimension, certainly is noteworthy) but also to the whole field of technologically implicated, commercially tainted, mass-produced cultural artifacts (boleros and tangos, radio soap operas, detective fiction, popular magazines, newspapers, the *novela rosa*, and science fiction, to name a few) that courses through his entire oeuvre. And these "texts" in turn evoke a universe of melodrama and cliché whose precise function and meaning, in their deracinated and resituated state, remain indeterminate. Neither parodic critique nor earnest homage, but a bit of both or neither, Puig's writing as a whole fleshes out surprising depth from a world of pure surface.

In *Betrayed by Rita Hayworth* Puig introduces a mode of writing that represents a new departure for the Spanish American novel, a mode embodying what we have called a "poetics of the prosaic." That poetics entails an apparently pedestrian registering of the everyday events and speech of ordinary, culturally dependent, and linguistically alienated characters. Within such a context, absence appears as a formal precept with respect both to plot development (there is no conventional continuity, climax, or final closure) and to narrative technique (consisting of a kaleidophone of first-person voices). The missing omniscient narrator constitutes an extension of and response to the absent paternal figure in the Oedipal drama enacted discontinuously among the main characters. In this sense, *Betrayed by Rita Hayworth* reveals itself to be an autobiographical novel in an uncommonly strong sense, for the youthful protagonist's behavior determines and explains the adult author's actions. As the novel's title indicates, moreover, deceit figures prominently in the narrative scheme, both on an intersubjective level (the characters betray one another with considerable frequency) and on that of the West's culture industry (Hollywood's fantasy fare instills illusions that underscore the humdrum pace of provincial life).

Heartbreak Tango: A Serial extends the inquiry into mass-culture behavior in the form of a mock tragedy based on gender- and genre-bound thinking. Within the bogus framework of a serial romance (combined with abundant doses of mystery fiction elements and bolero or tango lyrics), the novel relates a tale of almost ubiquitous sentimental failure, owing to the characters' uncritical conformity to sex-role stereotypes. Juan Carlos, the tubercular womanizer, and Pancho, the brawny laborer and patrolman, prove to be as dependent on Nené and Mabel for sociopsychological redemption as the women are on the men – and as much their conventional objects of desire. Only the proletarian Fanny escapes relatively unscathed from the trap of Manichean logic, not because she understands the more refined notion of gender and genre as points of discursive engenderment but because, true to the formula of serial romance, she is the only one to remain virtuous and untreasonous in a fallen world.

Without abandoning the motif of commercial film, *The Buenos Aires Affair: A Detective Novel* makes intensified use of pop psychoanalysis and defamiliarized pornography within an effaced mystery-fiction paradigm. Relative to *Heartbreak Tango* this novel engages in hyperbole on a number of fronts. Protagonists Leo and Gladys no longer merely conform to mainstream gender roles; their behavior is grotesquely conventional (he the sadistically macho critic, she the masochistically submissive artiste). Sex acquires for them a monolithic salience, and their dysfunctional sexuality occasions disastrous consequences. As in *Rita Hayworth*, Freudian psychoanalysis, especially as concerns the centrality of human sexuality, plays a major role in elaborating the text. But the sexual explanation for all the characters' woes is so pat that the Freudian model (or its application on a mass scale) comes into question. The Oedipal parricide in this instance is thus perpetrated against Freud himself, a challenge to authority reflected also in the absence of a clearly defined crime or even a detective figure (other than the reader) in this *soi-disant* detective novel.

The poetics of the prosaic noted in *Rita Hayworth* reaches new levels of austerity in *Kiss of the Spider Woman*, where characters (basically two) and setting (a prison cell) are pared down to a minimum for heightened dramatic intensity. In place of a narrator (here a transparency), moreover, the novel represents directly the interlocutors' utterances, allowing a relativized authorial voice to enter only in a series of footnotes that in turn dialogues with the characters' colloquy. The motif of betrayal, never really absent from Puig's fiction, reemerges prominently as Molina and Valentín vie duplicitously to manipulate each other and (vainly) the State. Within this acclaimed novel a number of powerful motifs (homosexuality as social practice, revolution as political practice, and run-of-the-mill movies as cultural practice) interact through writing to provide an especially sensitive and well-integrated account of the status of freedom in Argentina at the three-quarter century mark. One finds here also the most elaborate development of Puig's quasimystical notion of intersubjectivity, a mixture of altruism and alterity in which the metaphor "I am you" acquires literal value.

Consistent with the erosion of boundaries between subject and object implicit in the above formulation, *Pubis Angelical* features a foregrounded notion of erasure in the construction of a self, a society, and a text. Focusing on the erasure motif highlights patterns that might otherwise go undetected, such as the effacement of the omniscient narrator in *Spider Woman* and *Rita Hayworth*, the erosion of simple male/female oppositions and genre boundaries in *The Buenos Aires Affair* and *Heartbreak Tango*, and the blurring of distinctions between high culture and popular culture in all Puig's novels. Using a variety of modalities of writing (imaginary-symbolic narratives modeled after the *novela rosa* in the past and science fiction in the future; mimetic representations of journal writing and spontaneous speech in the present), *Pubis Angelical* extends the list of effaced dualities to include the political right and left as well as the opposition between nature and culture in gender definition. It chronicles Ana's search for knowledge, which although only partially successful results in felicitous reunion with other significant women in her life. Through the interaction of the diverse writings, human identity emerges as a construct that, if not entirely fathomable, may still yield well-being to the determined searcher.

In *Eternal Curse on the Reader of These Pages* the erasure figure is turned upon itself, textualized, and deflected toward an infernal register. Initially the transcription of a series of conversations the author had in English, the novel severely undermines the common-sense distinction between an original and its translation. The inter-locutors Larry and Ramírez constitute a difficult pair of *manqué* subjects who need each other to overcome their respective psychic repression, to erase their mental erasures. Larry's decoding of Ramírez's notebooks promises to provide access both to Ramírez's past and to Larry's future, restoring the men to psychic wholeness. But Larry's belief in the inevitability of an Oedipal scenario and Ramírez's residual paranoia and failing health conspire to thwart the potentially symbiotic process. Ramírez dies, partially because of Larry's intervention; Larry emerges partially castrated from his encounter with Ramírez. Both the native New Yorker and the Argen-tinean exile remain estranged from their environment and from themselves, accursed readers of their own partially erased psychic texts. Mutual betrayal leads to a dystopian conclusion in this further rewriting/erasure of the Oedipal narrative.

My strategy regarding Puig's last two novels was to show them to be not so much symptoms of the author's decline as inquiries into the trope of decline as a rhetorical device. In *Blood of Requited Love*, the indigent narrator-protagonist Josemar, unable to comply with the macho code imposed through the popular music of Roberto Carlos, must invent for himself a story of decline in the past to bol-ster his flagging ego in the present. Based on a primal scene of deflo-ration and rife with contradictory claims of triumph and unexplained aversions, Josemar's technically innovative narrative proposes de-cline as a curiously positive sign, for in order to have fallen one has to have been riding high once, right? As he keeps annihilation at bay, he raises epistemological questions of unprecedented proportions, for the relativity of truth, long a hallmark of Puig's fiction, in Jose-mar's neurotic discourse approaches a nullity. The protagonist's un-stable identity shows the name Josemar to be misleading, an empty signifier, a facade over a void of self-betrayal.

Tropical Night Falling similarly treats decline as a topos, a developmental stage or plot element that, in a classical setting, precedes death. As with any motif, however, that pattern is not immutable. Within an architecturally complex narrative scheme and a contrivedly exotic tropical setting, the novel's characters defamiliar-ize the cliché relation of decline and death, showing the truly inde-pendent status of each element. Some characters die suddenly, with no ostensible decline; others lead lives of seemingly permanent decline; and one, namely the irrepressible Nidia, stubbornly refuses to die and salvages an ascent from the jaws of almost certain decline. In this novel Puig projects himself with impressive vitality into an old age he himself would never know.

As I elaborated this study, which is so concerned with the multi-plicity of perceptions a single phenomenon can spawn, I was keenly aware of the arbitrary nature of the structure that was emerging. What would this book have looked like, I wondered, if I had studied Puig's works not according to the chronology of their publication but according to their proved commercial value or some other ratio-nal or irrational scheme? Further, what sorts of results would a study produce if it took the various approaches here employed and applied them to different texts by Puig? What follows is a series of fast-forward forays into the hypothetical book or books I did not write, this book's virtual Other.

The question of representing a moral problematics, for instance, raised here in connection with Puig's nonnovelistic fictions, could well apply to all his novels, both within and beyond the framework of betrayal and self-betrayal. Because treachery so pervades Puig's fictional world, the issue acquires greatest relief on those few occa-sions when the option to betray is eschewed, as in the case of the nonmasculine figures Mita in *Rita Hayworth*, Fanny in *Heartbreak Tango*, Molina in *Kiss of the Spider Woman*, and Ana in *Pubis Angel-ical*. The moral value of silence, whether enforced by governmental censorship (imposing one sector's view of morality on an entire populace) or by one's own internal repressive mechanism, promises to be a vein worth tapping. And whether the very popular culture that Puig always found irresistible is not in some measure maliciously duplicitous (democratic and demagogic) is another potentially fruit-ful avenue of inquiry. In particular, Puig's insistence on certain moral questions (intersubjective equality, guilt-free sex, etc.) within the context of both a trivialized divinity and a commodified artwork raises questions highly pertinent to a contemporary culture in which the Roman Catholic Church has begun marketing Dial-a-Pope messages for those who seek spiritual contact with the Holy Father.

The notion of decline, which arises in dealing with *Blood of Requited Love* and *Tropical Night Falling*, engenders a bipolar scheme when applied to Puig's other novels. On one extreme we have works like *Heartbreak Tango, The Buenos Aires Affair*, and *Eternal Curse*, all of which recount a "rise and fall" scenario. *Pubis Angelical* (along with the drama *Mystery of the Rose Bouquet*) stands opposite those works, inscribing an arc of "fall and rise." And somewhere in the middle ground we find *Rita Hayworth* (which, despite Mita's laments, never rises enough to fall and vice versa) and *Kiss of the Spider Woman* (which can be read as a victory, a defeat, or a draw, depending on the reader's cultural and ideological standpoint). What sets Puig apart from his contemporaries in this regard is the way he manages to insert attenuated glimpses of redemption into a fallen world that the meek shall not or would not want necessarily to inherit.

I have already spoken of some of the ways the motif of erasure applies to works beyond *Pubis Angelical* and *Eternal Curse*. It should be clear that Puig cannot be completely identified with the mass cultural artifacts he evokes because, regardless of his extratextual affection for them, he does not represent those artifacts in his texts without first tampering with them. By exaggerating, cutting, juxtaposing, and otherwise manipulating them, he blurs their boundaries and smudges the borders of the simplistic dualisms that form their conceptual bases. For most readers, I suspect the erasure that most readily catches the eye takes place at the site of narration. If *Rita Hayworth* caused a stir in the late 1960s with its "gallery" of nonauthoritarian first-person voices, works like *Kiss of the Spider Woman, Pubis Angelical, Eternal Curse*, and *Tropical Night Falling* go a good deal farther in representing voluntary self-effacement. The figure of the narrator in those works can be inferred only from its silence; it is a transparency we assume to be responsible for presenting the conversations we hear and the documents we read. Other ways Puig deauthorizes omniscience include the *nouveau roman*-like dispassionate description of surfaces and a robot-like, formulaic narration of external actions (*Heartbreak Tango*), a dubiously rational swerve of the camera-like narration from the matter at hand to a hypothetical or irrelevant detail (*The Buenos Aires Affair*), and a demented narrator whose insistence on omniscience and omni-potency invalidates the very discourse that makes those claims (*Blood of Requited Love*).

At this remove, the odd coupling proposed in regard to *Kiss of the Spider Woman* stands in sharp contrast to the "perfect" coupling of *The Buenos Aires Affair*'s sadistic Leo and masochistic Gladys. And this opposition acquires heightened relief when viewed in relation to the highly equivocal coupling of Josemar with Maria da Gloria in *Blood of Requited Love* and the "uncoupling" (degendering) figured in the oxymoronic title *Pubis Angelical*. Puig's fictions are full of characters trying to connect with others, of the same sex and of different sexes, of the same generation and of different generations, of the same ideology, class, and nationality and of different ideologies, classes, and nationalities. Some of these combinations succeed; most do not. The same may be said for the incongruous commingling in Puig's writing of what many consider to be cultural debris and matters of high seriousness. On both accounts Puig may be characterized as a heterodox experimenter, willing to take risks in order to make occasional gains. In view of the critical and public acclaim garnered by Puig's fourth novel, *Kiss of the Spider Woman*, unsympathetic readers could make the case that his coupling with the bricoleur's modus operandi resulted in an *ejaculatio praecox*.

Combining the critique of gender-bound and genre-determined thinking carried out in *The Buenos Aires Affair* and *Heartbreak Tango* with the absent-father syndrome figured in *Betrayed by Rita Hayworth*, I arrive at the following conclusions. Puig began his spectacular career by struggling with the dual straitjacket of sex-role definitions and notions of aesthetic decorum that were etched in stone. He continues to wage that struggle, which goes in search of a substitute for the paternal authority figure that dominates both those arenas, with every text he writes. Aware of the dangers of slavish obedience to a Freudian scenario (especially in *Eternal Curse* but also significantly in *Pubis Angelical*), he intellectualizes it, inverts it, bastardizes it, and tugs on its whiskers, but he never completely abandons the Oedipal scheme as a foundation for his textual worldview. The upshot is of course a hybrid doctrine, about as pure a psychoanalytical model as are his paradigms for genre and gender definitions. But purity is not necessarily a quality to prize in Puig's system, just as excessive denotation, which leaves little for the reader to imagine, constitutes another negative valence. In short, it is Puig's rejection of mastery as an authorial posture – preferring to labor with discarded and base cultural materials – and his skillful recuperation of orality within a mass-mediated neocolonial milieu that will likely mark his most enduring contribution to Latin American literature.

Notes and References

Preface

1. The "Boom" referred to denotes a period of unprecedented productivity in and worldwide recognition of the Latin American narrative that corresponds roughly with the decade of the 1960s. For three different accounts of this literary-commercial phenomenon see José Donoso, *The Boom in Spanish American Literature: A Personal History* (New York: Columbia University Press in association with the Center for Inter-American Relations, 1977); Emir Rodríguez Monegal, *El "boom" de la novela latinoamericana* (Caracas: Tiempo Nuevo, 1972); and Yvette E. Miller and Raymond Leslie Williams, eds., *The Boom in Retrospect: A Reconsideration*, a special issue of *Latin American Literary Review* 15, no. 29 (1987).

Chapter One

1. Two leading examples are Juan Francisco Manzano, *Autobiografía de un esclavo* (Autobiography of a slave) (1840; reprint, Madrid: Ediciones Guadarrama, 1975) and Anselmo Suárez y Romero, *Francisco, el ingenio; o, Las delicias del campo, novela cubana* (Francisco, the sugar mill; or, The delights of the countryside, a cuban novel) (1880; reprint, Havana: Ministerio de Educación, Dirección de Cultura, 1947).

2. This vast area is represented, reductively, by two principal authors, Mariano Azuela, in his *Los de abajo* (*The Underdogs*, 1916) and *La malhora* (The evil hour, 1923), and Martín Luis Guzmán, in his *El águila y la serpiente* (*The Eagle and the Serpent*, 1928) and *La sombra del caudillo* (The boss's shadow, 1929).

3. See the Selected Bibliography for complete data on Puig's novels, plays, and filmscripts, including English translations.

4. Bakhtin works out the notion of dialogism most thoroughly in *Problems of Dostoevsky's Poetics*, ed. and trans. Caryl Emerson, intro. Wayne C. Booth (1929; reprint, Minneapolis: University of Minnesota Press, 1984) and "Discourse in the Novel," in *The Dialogic Imagination: Four Essays*, ed. Michael Holquist, trans. Caryl Emerson and Michael Holquist (1935; reprint, Austin: University of Texas Press, 1981), 259-422. The inherent dialogism of novelistic prose finds its "Other" in the unitary language of lyric poetry, according to Bakhtin.

5. See especially the section titled "The Speaking Person in the Novel" in Bakhtin's essay "Discourse in the Novel," 330-55. I am grateful to

Roberto Echevarren for having suggested in "A partir de *Rita Hayworth*: Alteridad y heteroglosia," in *Manuel Puig: Montaje y alteridad del sujeto* (Manuel Puig: Montage and alterity of the subject) (Santiago, Chile: Monografías del Maitén, Instituto Profesional del Pacífico, 1986), 21, that "Manuel Puig's novels prove to be privileged ground for the study of heteroglossia in Bakhtin's strictest sense: the incorporation of socially charged speech into the text of the novel" (my translation).

6. *Bajo un manto de estrellas* (Barcelona: Seix Barral, 1983); translated as *Under a Mantle of Stars: A Play in Two Acts*, trans. Ronald Christ (New York: Lumen Books, 1985), 2. Parenthetical page references within text are to this edition.

Chapter Two

1. Page references that appear parenthetically are to *Betrayed by Rita Hayworth*, trans. Suzanne Jill Levine (New York: Vintage Books, 1981). When, on occasion, the published translation has not suited my purposes, I have so indicated.

2. The most refined depiction of the elusive author figure to date is given by Lucille Kerr, *Suspended Fictions: Reading Novels by Manuel Puig* (Urbana and Chicago: University of Illinois Press, 1987); hereafter cited in text. See especially pp. 55-72 and the concluding paragraphs of each chapter of textual commentary.

3. René A. Campos, *Espejos: La textura cinemática en "La traición de Rita Hayworth"* (Madrid: Pliegos, 1985), 48, identifies the Shirley Temple film as *The Little Colonel* (Twentieth-Century Fox, 1935). Campos's book is particularly valuable as an aid in deciphering the text's pervasive film motif.

4. According to Jorgelina Corbatta, *Mito personal y mitos colectivos en las novelas de Manuel Puig* (Madrid: Orígenes, 1988), this conflictive scenario constitutes Puig's "mito personal" (personal myth), the unconscious raw material from which the novel issues.

5. My translation from the original Spanish; the English translation omits the passage altogether.

6. Emir Rodríguez Monegal, "A Literary Myth Exploded," *Review 72* (Winter 1971-Spring 1972): 56-64.

7. Norman Lavers, *Pop Culture into Art: The Novels of Manuel Puig* (Columbia: University of Missouri Press, 1988), 21.

8. The English translation gives no indication of the novel's division into two parts of almost identical length – a significant omission in view of the battle of the sexes enacted between the last narrators of each part.

9. David R. Southard, *"Betrayed by Rita Hayworth*: Reader Deception and Anti-climax in His Novels," *Latin American Literary Review* 4, no. 9 (1976): 22-28. Puig employs this sort of detective-fiction scenario, with important variations, in his next two novels, *Heartbreak Tango* and *The*

Buenos Aires Affair. In that psychoanalysis also entails a similar tracing of clues in search of a solution, two other novels by Puig, *Eternal Curse on the Reader of These Pages* and *Blood of Requited Love,* also involve considerable sleuthing activity.

10. In the context of this argument, writing, which necessarily manipulates the pen, is tantamount to masturbation, an activity denied the "real" man.

Chapter Three

1. Jorge Luis Borges, *Ficciones,* ed. and intro. Anthony Kerrigan, trans. Anthony Bonner (New York: Grove Press, 1962), 45-55.

2. *Heartbreak Tango: A Serial,* trans. Suzanne Jill Levine (New York: Dutton, 1973); *The Buenos Aires Affair: A Detective Novel,* trans. Suzanne Jill Levine (New York: Dutton, 1976). The novels were published in the original Spanish as *Boquitas pintadas: Folletín* (Buenos Aires: Sudamericana, 1969) and *The Buenos Aires Affair: Novela policial* (Buenos Aires: Sudamericana, 1973), respectively. Page references are to the published English translations.

3. Julio Rodríguez-Luis, *"Boquitas pintadas:* ¿Folletín unanimista?," *Sin Nombre* 5 (1974): 50-56.

4. The discussion of the conventions of serial fiction owes much to the following studies: John G. Cawelti, *Adventure, Mystery, and Romance: Formula Stories as Art and Popular Culture* (Chicago and London: University of Chicago Press, 1976), 5-50; Emir Rodríguez Monegal, "El folletín rescatado," *Revista de la Universidad de México* 27 (October 1972): 25-35; Myrna Solotorevsky, *Literatura/Paraliteratura: Borges, Donoso, Cortázar, Vargas Llosa* (Gaithersburg, Md.: Hispamérica, 1988), 25-80; and Severo Sarduy, "Notas a las notas a las notas . . .: A propósito de Manuel Puig," *Revista Iberoamericana* 37 (1971): 555-67. Page references to these works are hereafter cited in text.

5. For a landmark analysis of the industrialization of art see Walter Benjamin, "The Work of Art in the Age of Mechanical Reproduction," in *Illuminations,* ed. and intro. Hannah Arendt, trans. Harry Zohn (New York: Schocken Books, 1969), 217-51.

6. The verb form of *entrega* is *entregar,* whose primary sense is "to submit," as when one yields one's body up to another, more powerful subject. The gender/genre dynamic thus pervades the text even at this elemental level.

7. I am persuaded by Jorgelina Corbatta's contention that the novel is not to be construed in reference to serial novels of the nineteenth century but rather to video or audio serials (i.e., television, film, or radio soap operas). The term *textuality* therefore should be taken here in an

expanded, figurative sense. See Jorgelina Corbatta, *Mito personal y mitos colectivos en las novelas de Manuel Puig* (Madrid: Orígenes, 1988), 36-37.

8. Elías Miguel Muñoz, *Discurso utópico de la sexualidad en Manuel Puig* (Madrid: Pliegos, 1987), is a prominent recent example.

9. Pamela Bacarisse, *The Necessary Dream: A Study of the Novels of Manuel Puig* (Cardiff: University of Wales Press, 1988), resorts to the oxymoron "non-distanced irony" (55) in attempting to explain the way in which Puig's texts resist a determination of their evaluative stance with regard to their own fictions.

10. The references here are to two fundamental works in the creation of "autonomous" characters, Luigi Pirandello, *Six Characters in Search of an Author*, in *Three Plays* (New York: Dutton, 1922); and Miguel de Unamuno y Jugo, *Niebla (Nivola)* (1914; reprint, Madrid: Espasa-Calpe, 1975).

11. See Kerr's discussion of the "perfect match" between the serial novel and the serial lover in *Suspended Fictions*, 94-105.

12. Marta Morello-Frosch, "La sexualidad opresiva en las obras de Manuel Puig," *Nueva Narrativa Hispánica* 5, nos. 1-2 (1975): 151-57.

13. This idea develops from the aforementioned study of David R. Southard, *"Betrayed by Rita Hayworth*: Reader Deception and Anti-climax in His Novels."

14. One of many examples would be Arthur Conan Doyle, *The Hound of the Baskervilles: Another Adventure of Sherlock Holmes* (New York: Grosset & Dunlap, 1902).

15. Geoffrey Hartman, "Literature High and Low," in *The Fate of Reading* (Chicago: University of Chicago Press, 1975), 203-22. The neologism appears on p. 206.

Chapter Four

1. Jack Kroll, "The Sound of Music: Off-off-off-Broadway," *Newsweek*, 14 May 1990, 73; hereafter cited in text.

2. "Milestones," *Newsweek*, 6 August 1990, 72.

3. Original publication data: Barcelona, Seix Barral, 1976. Film data: *Kiss of the Spider Woman* (1985). Director: Héctor Babenco. Starring: William Hurt, Raúl Juliá, and Sonia Braga. The English translation to which I refer was rendered by Thomas Colchie (New York: Vintage Books, 1980).

4. In addition to those genres already mentioned, there exists a theatrical version of *El beso de la mujer araña* (Barcelona: Seix Barral, 1983) that has been performed throughout the Spanish-speaking world and beyond (for a brief analysis of which see chapter 7). English version: *The Kiss of the Spider Woman*, in *Drama Contemporary: Latin America – Plays by Manuel Puig, Antonio Skármeta, Mario Vargas Llosa, Carlos Fuentes*, ed. George W. Woodyard and Marion Peter Hold, English adaptation by Michael Feingold (New York: PAJ Publications, 1986), 19-61.

5. This statement reflects a broad array of readings in postmodern culture. For analyses of the more nihilistic aspects of the phenomenon, consult Jean Baudrillard, *In the Shadow of the Silent Majorities, or The Death of the Social*, trans. Paul Foss, Paul Patton, and John Johnston (New York: Semiotext[e], 1983), and Arthur Kroker and David Cook, *The Postmodern Scene: Excremental Culture and Hyper-Aesthetics* (New York: St. Martin's Press, 1986).

6. Michael Wood, "The Claims of Mischief," *New York Review of Books*, 24 January 1980, 43-47.

7. Marcelo Coddou, "Seis preguntas a Manuel Puig sobre su última novela: *El beso de la mujer araña*," *American Hispanist* 18 (May 1977): 12-13.

8. Here again we depend on the author's spoken word. See Ronald Christ, "A Last Interview with Manuel Puig," *World Literature Today* 65, no. 4 (1991): 571-78, with pertinent passages appearing on pp. 573-74.

9. These are *Crónicas de Bustos Domecq*, *Seis problemas para don Isidro Parodi*, and *Nuevos cuentos de Bustos Domecq*.

10. Amnesty International reports, for instance, the following damning information about Colombia, a country that has had only one military coup in the twentieth century and is generally perceived as showing respect for the institutions of democracy: "Among those who continue to be harassed, illegally detained, tortured, and summarily executed, are members of the Communist Party and Patriotic Union, trade unionists, teachers, religious personnel, and members of indigenous and other marginalized groups in Colombian society" (*Colombia Update* 1, no. 4 [1989]: 1).

11. For a hyperbolic but provocative metaphysical account of the flattened emptiness of existence in the computer age, see Jean Baudrillard, *Simulations*, trans. Paul Foss, Paul Patton, and Philip Beitchman (New York: Semiotext[e], 1983).

12. I allude to Baudrillard, *In the Shadow of the Silent Majorities* (see note 5 of this chapter).

13. See my "Order, Chaos, and Re-order: The Fiction of Manuel Puig," *Kentucky Romance Quarterly* 30, 2 (1983): 187-201.

14. The lack of a narrator to reveal background material regarding the characters or their circumstances occasions this odd coupling: the novel, although profoundly political, is practically ahistorical. Other than what one can glean from the interlocutors' utterances, it has no explicit past.

15. The novel transpires over an indeterminate period of weeks in 1975. Both prisoners are transferred to their cell on 4 April of that year. The last date mentioned, the day of Molina's death, is Friday, the 25th of some undisclosed month (this comes via a police report [273]). That month is presumably not April, as the profound changes the characters undergo could not plausibly take place in so compressed a time span.

16. Julio Cortázar, *Rayuela* (Buenos Aires: Sudamericana, 1963).

17. Lloyd S. Kramer, "Literature, Criticism, and Historical Imagination: The Literary Challenge of Hayden White and Dominick LaCapra," in *The New Cultural History*, ed. Lynn Hunt (Berkeley and Los Angeles: University of California Press, 1989): 97-130.

Chapter Five

1. Lucille Kerr, "The Dis-appearance of a Popular Author: Stealing around Style with Manuel Puig's *Pubis angelical*," in *Figuring the Author: Recent Fiction from Spanish America* (Durham: Duke University Press, 1992).

2. Original publication data are *Pubis angelical* (Barcelona: Seix Barral, 1979) and *Maldición eterna a quien lea estas páginas* (Barcelona: Seix Barral, 1980). Page references in this chapter are to the following English-language editions: *Pubis Angelical*, trans. Elena Brunet (New York: Vintage Books, 1986), and *Eternal Curse on the Reader of These Pages* (New York: Random House, 1982). Note the seven-year delay in publishing the translation of *Pubis angelical*, initially perceived as a pale sequel to *Kiss of the Spider Woman*.

3. For an assortment of Lacan's most influential texts in English, see Jacques Lacan, *Ecrits: A Selection*, trans. Alan Sheridan (New York: Norton, 1977). A helpful secondary source is Benvenuto Rice and Roger Kennedy, *The Works of Jacques Lacan: An Introduction* (New York: St. Martin's Press, 1986).

4. Pamela Bacarisse, *The Necessary Dream: A Study of the Novels of Manuel Puig* (Cardiff: University of Wales Press, 1988), 128.

5. George Yúdice, "*El beso de la mujer araña* y *Pubis angelical*: entre el placer y el saber," in *Literature and Popular Culture in the Hispanic World*, ed. Rose S. Minc (Gaithersburg, Md.: Hispamérica, 1981), 43-57.

6. Elías Miguel Muñoz, *El discurso utópico de la sexualidad en Manuel Puig* (Madrid: Editorial Pliegos, 1987), 102 (my translation).

7. See (if you must) Hedy Lamarr, *Ecstasy and Me: My Life as a Woman* (New York: Bartholomew House, 1966), 111-87.

8. Myrna Solotorevsky, *Literatura/Paraliteratura: Puig, Borges, Donoso, Cortázar, Vargas Llosa* (Gaithersburg, Md.: Hispamérica, 1988), 25.

9. Puig's own statements on sexuality do not indicate the tendency toward puritanical repression that a literal reading of *Pubis Angelical*'s master trope might seem to indicate. In an interview with Jorgelina Corbatta he advocates not homosexuality but, at the very least, bisexuality, if not omnisexuality (something akin to Freud's notion of "polymorphous perversity," in which the subject does not channel sexuality into the geni-

tals but is capable of sexual feeling throughout the body). See Christ, "Interview with Manuel Puig."

10. Jorgelina Corbatta, *Mito personal y mitos colectivos en las novelas de Manuel Puig* (Madrid: Orígenes, 1988), 89-91, provides excerpts from an interview with the author that explain how the novel is based on a series of conversations Puig had in English with a young man in New York. The "original" language of the novel is therefore not, in this case, Spanish (note there is no translator listed regarding the English version). Some critics have complained about the unpolished style of the Spanish, which includes literal renditions of such colloquial English expressions as *"boca de trinchera"* (trench mouth), *"reductores de cabeza"* (shrinks), and *"cabeza de huevo"* (egghead).

11. The sequences in which the "collective dreaming" takes place are 56-60, 64-66, 84-91, 96-101, and 106-9 (part 1) and 126-31, 134-38, 154-56, and 167-78 (part 2).

12. Before Larry's family name was changed, it was Giovanangelo (John Angel, see *Eternal Curse*, 22). The combining of his original name with his sexual impotence yields the conclusion that he is a male version of the ideally unsexed subject ciphered in *Pubis Angelical*.

13. An utterly new departure for Puig in *Eternal Curse* is the avoidance of a 16-chapter format, a structuring device to which he remained faithful throughout his first five novels. Whereas the novel is still divided into two parts of similar length, the sections that make up each part are of unequal and unpredictable extension. As a result of this change the novel bears less of a formal resemblance to mass-produced literature than any of Puig's previous works. Theme and form, once again, to the extent they can be separated, work in consonance.

14. Ramírez's "internal dialogues" appear on 15-19 and 51-52 (part 1) and 84-91, 157-63, 189-95, and 221-23 (part 2). There are no corresponding sequences for Larry.

Chapter Six

1. Jean-François Lyotard, *The Postmodern Condition: A Report on Knowledge*, trans. Geoff Bennington and Brian Massumi, foreword by Fredric Jameson (Minneapolis: University of Minnesota Press, 1983).

2. The original texts are *Sangre de amor correspondido* (Barcelona: Seix Barral, 1982) and *Cae la noche tropical* (Barcelona: Seix Barral, 1988). The translations referred to parenthetically in this chapter are *Blood of Requited Love*, trans. Jan L. Grayson (New York: Vintage, 1984), and *Tropical Night Falling*, trans. Suzanne Jill Levine (New York: Simon and Schuster, 1991). I wish to thank Suzanne Jill Levine and Marie Arana-Ward for allowing me access to the advance uncorrected proofs of *Tropical Night Falling*.

3. Jorge Campos, "Dos novelas recientes," *Insula* 37, 428-29 (1982): 18, associates *Blood of Requited Love* with a thematic subgenre he calls "*la novela de la pobreza*" (the poverty novel).

4. For a study of repetition in the novel see René Campos, "El recuento en *Sangre de amor correspondido*," *Chasqui* 18, no. 2 (1989): 36-42. An analysis of the motif of narcissism may be found in Flora Schiminovich, "Juego narcisista y ficcional en *Sangre de amor correspondido*," *Discurso Literario* 1, no. 2 (1984): 295-301.

5. Josemar's disgust upon seeing Maria da Gloria's blood may indicate his uneasiness with the oppressor's role he attempts to adopt. Likewise, his fear of snakes could be taken as an unconscious rejection of the sexual aggressiveness with which he attributes himself. These dissonant elements, like the first-person voices that interrupt his seemingly authoritative and objective narrative, refuse to disappear, requiring him to retell his tale again and again.

6. The novel's biblical and patriarchal underpinnings are exposed by Elías Miguel Muñoz, "El discurso del poder judeocristiano en *Sangre de amor correspondido*," in *El discurso utópico de la sexualidad en Manuel Puig* (Madrid: Pliegos, 1987), 107-30. It is not irrelevant to the present analysis that Adam and Eve, pictured on the cover of the novel's original edition, suffer a fall from grace analogous to the one Josemar evokes verbally.

7. Just how skeptical one "ought to be" is a disquieting question. Should elements such as the seduction be accepted as true just because they are tawdry and insistently reiterated? What about Josemar's children? Did he "really" sire them, or are they merely part of his will to manliness (he appears to engender them with the same lack of accountability that characterizes his use of language in general; maybe they are a typical product of that language run amok)? Delving more radically, was there ever a Maria da Gloria? Why does asking that question threaten to portray Josemar as "too" demented?

8. Jorgelina Corbatta, *Mito personal y mitos colectivos en las novelas de Manuel Puig* (Madrid: Orígenes, 1988), 104, describes this phenomenon as a "dialogue of voices in first and third person, which takes place in the mind of the protagonist as projections of a doubled self, debating between the real and the imaginary" (my translation).

9. Given the extreme fragility of Josemar's identity, Jorge Campos (see note 3 of this chapter) considers the protagonist of the novel to be memory itself. Corbatta (see note 8) considers Josemar to be both "actor and stage" (my translation).

10. A thinly veiled reference to the one-time cult novel by Richard Fariña, *Been Down So Long It Looks Like Up to Me* (New York: Random House, 1966).

11. See Jorge Luis Borges, "The Immortal," in *Labyrinths: Selected Stories and Other Writings*, ed. Donald A. Yates and James E. Irby, trans. James

E. Irby, preface by André Maurois (New York: New Directions, 1962), 105-18, among others, for his notion of the identity of all authors (e.g., Homer = St. Augustine = Cervantes = Joyce). See also "Homenaje a César Paladión" (Homage to César Paladión), in Jorge Luis Borges and Adolfo Bioy Casares, *Crónicas de Bustos Domecq* (Chronicles of Bustos Domecq) (Buenos Aires: Losada, 1967), 15-20, for a whimsical defense of the originality of plagiarism.

12. These comments are made within a rationalist and existentialist framework. Despite the sisters' attachment to numerous traditional notions, neither one can bring herself to believe in an afterlife. See their statements on pp. 25, 49, 102, and 126.

13. Luci's behavior regarding topics of prurient interest is touchingly inconsistent. She tends to suppress any direct reference to matters of carnal knowledge, euphemizing the sex act (much like Josemar in *Blood of Requited Love*) as "it" (20), "the inevitable" (78), and a "tumble in the hay" (98), maintaining nonetheless an acute interest in all things related to the taboo subject. Nidia, for her part, cannot refer to the relatively liberated Silvia without resorting to circumlocution or attaching some sort of epithet to her name: she is "the woman next door" (19), "that girl" (29), "this Silvia" (17), and "your Silvia" (113). Despite the disapproval implicit in these sobriquets, Nidia's keen interest in Silvia runs parallel to Luci's fascination with an eroticism so powerful it is unnameable.

14. Julio Cortázar, *All Fires the Fire*, trans. Suzanne Jill Levine (New York: Pantheon, 1973), 30-48.

15. The Zen Buddhist *koan*, or problematical subject for reflection, most often cited is "What is the sound of one hand clapping?"

16. According to Pamela Bacarisse's "Necrología" (Obituary) for the author in *Revista Iberoamericana* 56, nos. 152-53 (1990): 1365-70, Puig's last four novels have been "rather neglected" (1368, my translation). During a survey conducted in July 1991, in which I consulted recent issues of the usual specialized journals (*Chasqui, Crítica Hispánica, Discurso Literario, Dispositio, Hispania, Hispanic Review, Nuevo Texto Crítico*) and of the literary supplements of several leading Latin American newspapers (*Journal de Brasil* [Rio de Janeiro], *El Mercurio* [Santiago, Chile], *El Nacional* [Caracas], *El Tiempo* [Bogotá], *El Comercio* [Lima], and *Excelsior* [Mexico City]), I was able to find only one brief and tepid journalistic review of the *Tropical Night Falling*, by María Adela Renard in *La Prensa* (Buenos Aires), 12 February 1989, 2. The novel had already been published for five months by the time the review appeared. An article on the novel, mostly descriptive of plot elements, finally did appear in the United States in fall 1991; see Michael DuPouy, "Brazilian Nights, Argentine Voices: *Tropical Night Falling*," *Review of Contemporary Fiction* 11, no. 3 (1991): 246-51.

17. Adolfo Bioy Casares, *Diary of the War of the Pig: A Novel*, trans. Gregory Woodruff and Donald A. Yates (New York: McGraw-Hill, 1972), and Gabriel García Márquez, *Love in the Time of Cholera*, trans. Edith Grossman (New York: Knopf, 1988), are two contemporary Spanish American novels that not only treat sustainedly the theme of old age but do so with marked compassion.

Chapter Seven

1. All the following texts are authored by Manuel Puig: *Under a Mantle of Stars*, cited in note 6, chapter 1. *El beso de la mujer araña: Adaptación escénica de la novela homónima de Manuel Puig, realizada por el autor*, in *Bajo un manto de estrellas* (Barcelona: Seix Barral, 1983). *La cara del villano/Memoria de Tijuana* (Barcelona: Seix Barral, 1985). *Mystery of the Rose Bouquet*, trans. Allan Baker (London: Faber and Faber, 1988). Parenthetical page references within the text are to these editions. Translations, where published translations are unavailable, are my own.

2. This chapter was cast in its present form largely in response to a eulogistic article by the Spanish novelist Juan Goytisolo, "On Being Morally Correct," *Review of Contemporary Fiction* 11, no. 3 (1991): 186-88. The piece originally appeared as an obituary in *El País* (Madrid), 27 July 1990. Labeling an action as "politically correct" in the United States has become the Right's way of dismissing (typically progressive) action as mere conformity. Not by accident, the intrinsic merit of the stigmatized behavior is thus often overlooked. Needless to say, my appropriation of Goytisolo's formulation does not reflect such a perspective on Puig's work. On the contrary, I seek, in addition to recognizing the affinities between the displaced Spaniard and the wandering Argentine, to underline Puig's nonconformist stance as regards moral content in contemporary art. Another Spaniard who has observed the moral cast of Puig's fiction is Pere Gimferrer, "Aproximaciones a Manuel Puig," *Plural* 57 (June 1976): 21-25.

3. The other drama by Puig published in English translation is *Mystery of the Rose Bouquet*. In addition, the original cinematographic version of *Kiss of the Spider Woman* (1985) was filmed in English.

4. In one of the very few articles of criticism published on this drama, Gabriela Mora, "Un problema de la pragmática del texto teatral: El nivel del acotador en *Bajo un manto de estrellas* de Manuel Puig," *Dispositio* 12, nos. 33-35 (1988): 223-33, contends Puig goes too far in shaking the foundations of the Real. By giving the explicit author a sometimes melodramatic, sometimes inscrutable voice, Puig has fashioned a radically indeterminate, confusing text.

5. Wolfgang Iser, *The Act of Reading: A Theory of Aesthetic Response* (Baltimore: Johns Hopkins University Press, 1978).

6. Elías Miguel Muñoz, "Show and Tell: Notes on Puig's Theater," *Review of Contemporary Fiction* 11, no. 3 (1991): 252-57. See also "The

Dramatic Triangle of Manuel Puig," *Los Angeles Times*, 16 November 1989, F1, F8.

7. See Puig's prologue, p. 11. Jorgelina Corbatta quotes this passage in "The Fantastic in Puig," *World Literature Today* 65, no. 4 (1991): 600n15.

8. Umberto Eco, *Postscript to "The Name of the Rose"* (San Diego: Harcourt Brace Jovanovich, 1988), 3. I am grateful to Puig's most prolific translator, Suzanne Jill Levine, for having brought this citation to my attention. See her *The Subversive Scribe: Translating Latin American Fiction* (Saint Paul, Minn.: Graywolf Press, 1991), 117n5.

9. In Winston Leyland, ed. *My Deep Dark Pain Is Love: A Collection of Latin American Gay Fiction*, trans. E. A. Lacey (San Francisco: Gay Sunshine Press, 1983), 71-76.

10. "The Usual Suspects," trans. Alfred MacAdam, *Review: Latin American Literature and Arts* (January-June 1991): 75-77. Reprinted from *Chorus* 8 (September 1990): 152-53.

11. "Vivaldi: A Screenplay," *Review of Contemporary Fiction* 11, no. 3 (1991): 177-81.

12. "Relative Humidity 95%," in *A Hammock beneath the Mangoes: Stories from Latin America*, ed. Thomas Colchie, trans. Andrew Hurley (New York: Dutton, 1991), 68-77. For a rare listing of Puig's unpublished works, including several screen and television scripts and proposals, see Patricia Bacarisse, "The Uses of Culture," *Review of Contemporary Fiction* 11, no. 3 (1991): 197-207. See especially note 2 on p. 207.

13. Puig had unsuccessfully tried to convince Suzanne Jill Levine to take on the project and so decided to write the script directly in English himself. See Ilan Stavans, "Good-Bye to M.P.," *Review of Contemporary Fiction* 11, no. 3 (1991): 159-64, and Suzanne Jill Levine, "Manuel Puig Exits Laughing," *Review of Contemporary Fiction* 11, no. 3 (1991): 190-96.

14. See note 2 of this chapter.

Selected Bibliography

PRIMARY WORKS

Spanish Editions

Novels

El beso de la mujer araña. Barcelona: Seix Barral, 1976.
Boquitas pintadas: Folletín. Buenos Aires: Sudamericana, 1969.
The Buenos Aires Affair: Novela policial. Buenos Aires: Sudamericana, 1973.
Cae la noche tropical. Barcelona: Seix Barral, 1988.
Maldición eterna a quien lea estas páginas. Barcelona: Seix Barral, 1980.
Pubis angelical. Barcelona: Seix Barral, 1979.
Sangre de amor correspondido. Barcelona: Seix Barral, 1982.
La traición de Rita Hayworth. Buenos Aires. Jorge Alvarez, 1968.

Other

Bajo un manto de estrellas: Pieza en dos actos/El beso de la mujer araña: Adaptación escénica por el autor. Barcelona: Seix Barral, 1983. (Plays.)
La cara del villano/Recuerdo de Tijuana. Barcelona: Seix Barral, 1985. (Screenplays.)

English Translations

Novels

Betrayed by Rita Hayworth. Translated by Suzanne Jill Levine. New York: Dutton, 1971.
Blood of Requited Love. Translated by Jan L. Grayson. New York: Vintage, 1984.
The Buenos Aires Affair: A Detective Novel. Translated by Suzanne Jill Levine. New York: Dutton, 1976.
Eternal Curse on the Reader of These Pages. Translated by the author. New York: Random House, 1982.
Heartbreak Tango: A Serial. Translated by Suzanne Jill Levine. New York: Dutton, 1973. (Translation of *Boquitas pintadas*.)

Kiss of the Spider Woman. Translated by Thomas Colchie. New York: Knopf, 1979.

Pubis Angelical. Translated by Elena Brunet. New York: Vintage, 1986.

Tropical Night Falling. Translated by Suzanne Jill Levine. New York: Simon & Schuster, 1991.

Other

"The Black Detective," "The Sado-Masoch Blues," and "Classical Farrah." In *My Deep Dark Pain Is Love: A Collection of Gay Fiction*, edited by Winston Leyland, translated by E. A. Lacey, 71-76. San Francisco: Gay Sunshine, 1983. (Short stories.)

The Kiss of the Spider Woman. In *Drama Contemporary: Latin America– Plays by Manuel Puig, Antonio Skármeta, Mario Vargas Llosa, Carlos Fuentes*, edited by George W. Woodyard and Marion Peter Holt, 19-61. English adaptation by Michael Feingold. New York: PAJ Publications, 1986. (Play version.)

Kiss of the Spider Woman: The Screenplay. Adapted by Leonard Schrader. Boston: Faber & Faber, 1987.

Mystery of the Rose Bouquet. Translated by Allan J. Baker. Boston and London: Faber & Faber, 1988.

"Relative Humidity 95%." In *A Hammock Beneath the Mangoes: Stories from Latin America*, edited by Thomas Colchie, translated by Andrew Hurley, 66-77. New York: Dutton, 1991. (Short story.)

Under a Mantle of Stars: A Play in Two Acts. Translated by Ronald Christ. New York: Lumen, 1985.

"The Usual Suspects." Translated by Alfred J. MacAdam. *Review: Latin American Literature and the Arts* (January-June 1991): 75-77. (Story originally published in *Chorus* [Rome] 8 [September 1990]: 152-53.)

SECONDARY WORKS

Books

Bacarisse, Pamela. *The Necessary Dream: A Study of the Novels of Manuel Puig.* Cardiff: University of Wales Press, 1988 (U.S. edition: Totowa, N.J.: Barnes & Noble, 1988). Treats Puig's novels by bringing a wealth of factual data to the individual readings.

_____. *Impossible Choices: The Implications of Cultural References in the Novels of Manuel Puig.* Forthcoming. Elaborates upon the many cultural allusions, popular and "serious," in Puig's novels.

Bakhtin, Mikhail M. *The Dialogic Imagination: Four Essays.* Edited by Michael Holquist, translated by Caryl Emerson and Michael Holquist. 1935. Reprint. Austin: University of Texas Press, 1981. Contains "Epic and Novel," "From the Prehistory of Novelistic Discourse," "Forms of

Time and of the Chronotope in the Novel," and "Discourse in the Novel." Enormously influential studies on narrative discourse and the source for such key concepts as dialogism, heteroglossia, polyphony, and chronotope.

_____. *Problems of Dostoevsky's Poetics.* Edited and translated by Caryl Emerson, introduction by Wayne C. Booth. 1929. Reprint. Minneapolis: University of Minnesota Press, 1984. Develops notion of "autonomous characters" along with dialogism, polyphony, and other aspects of narrative discourse as seen in Dostoevsky's fiction.

Campos, René Alberto. *Espejos: La textura cinemática en "La traición de Rita Hayworth."* Madrid: Pliegos, 1985. Lacanian-inspired investigation into the film motif in Puig's first novel; features a *"filmografía"* of cinematic references.

Corbatta, Jorgelina. *Mito personal y mitos colectivos en las novelas de Manuel Puig.* Madrid: Orígenes, 1988. A sociopsychoanalytical approach to Puig's fiction, interwoven with fragments of interviews between the critic and the author.

Donoso, José. *The Boom in Spanish American Literature: A Personal History.* New York: Columbia University Press in association with the Center for Inter-American Relations, 1977. An insider's view of the novelistic "Boom" on whose fringe Puig's writing perches.

Echavarren, Roberto, and Enrique Giordano. *Manuel Puig: Montaje y alteridad del sujeto.* Santiago, Chile: Monografías del Maitén, Instituto Profesional del Pacífico, 1986. An ensemble of refined essays by alternating coauthors on diverse aspects of Puig's novels (except *Pubis Angelical*), unified by a questioning of self-presence in writing and personal identity.

García Ramos, Juan Manuel. *La narrativa de Manuel Puig (Por una crítica en libertad).* Santa Cruz de Tenerife, Canary Islands: Universidad de La Laguna, 1982. A published doctoral dissertation that, once beyond its long-winded theoretical introduction, provides useful insights into the novels up to *Eternal Curse.*

Kerr, Lucille. *Suspended Fictions: Reading Novels by Manuel Puig.* Urbana: University of Illinois Press, 1987. The most rigorous study on Puig to date, an analysis of the many insoluble indeterminacies of the first four novels.

Lavers, Norman. *Pop Culture into Art: The Novels of Manuel Puig.* Columbia: University of Missouri Press, 1988. Occasionally suggestive, brief essays by a non-Hispanist.

Muñoz, Elías Miguel. *El discurso utópico de la sexualidad en Manuel Puig.* Madrid: Pliegos, 1987. Casts Puig's oeuvre, up to *Blood of Requited Love* and bracketing *Eternal Curse*, as centered around the verbal representation of sexuality.

Pauls, Alan. *Manuel Puig: La traición de Rita Hayworth*. Buenos Aires: Hachette, 1986. Reconstructs the atmosphere of Argentina in the 1960s, when Puig was writing his first novel.

Rodríguez Monegal, Emir. *El "boom" de la novela latinoamericana*. Caracas: Tiempo Nuevo, 1972. An authoritative account of Latin America's novelistic "Boom" by the critic (and editor of the influential Parisian journal *Mundo Nuevo*, 1966-71) who most promoted it.

Solotorevsky, Myrna. *Literatura/paraliteratura: Puig, Borges, Donoso, Cortázar, Vargas Llosa*. Gaithersburg, Md.: Hispamérica, 1988. A Bakhtin-derived study of the mass-culture dimension of works by the authors named, especially Puig.

Steinberg de Kaplan, Olga Ruth. *Manuel Puig: Un innovador de la novela argentina*. Tucumán, Argentina: Universidad Nacional de Tucumán, Secretaría de Extensión Universitaria, 1989. Studies Puig's writing within an Argentine national context.

Articles, Bibliographies, Interviews, and Parts of Books

Benjamin, Walter. "The Work of Art in the Age of Mechanical Reproduction." In *Illuminations*, edited and with an introduction by Hannah Arendt, translated by Harry Zohn, 217-52. New York: Schocken Books, 1969. Seminal piece on the work of art's loss of "aura" in the industrial age. A basic text for popular culture and postmodernist studies.

Borinsky, Alicia. "Castración y lujos: La escritura de Manuel Puig." *Revista Iberoamericana* 90 (January-March 1975), 29-45. An important study regarding the need to rethink cultural categories and hierarchies of discourse.

Chamberlin, Lori. "The Subject in Exile: Puig's *Eternal Curse*." *Novel* 20, no. 3 (1977): 260-75. Sensitive and thorough poststructural analysis of the exile motif.

Christ, Ronald. "A Last Interview with Manuel Puig." *World Literature Today* 65, no. 4 (1991): 571-78. Especially helpful in construing the potential effects of *Kiss of the Spider Woman*.

Clark, David Draper. "Manuel Puig: Selected Bibliography." *World Literature Today* 65, no. 4 (1991): 655-62. Updating of previous bibliographies compiled by Pamela Bacarisse, Jorgelina Corbatta, Juan Armando Epple, Angel Flores, and David W. Foster.

Freud, Sigmund. *The Interpretation of Dreams*. Translated and edited by James Strachey. New York: Avon, 1965. See pp. 294-97. Freud's first published discussion (ca. 1900) of the Oedipus complex.

_____. Letter #71, 3 October 1897. In *Origins of Psycho-Analysis: Letters to Wilhelm Fleiss, Drafts and Notes: 1887-1902*, edited by Marie Bonaparte, Anna Freud, and Ernst Kris; translated by Eric Mosbacher and James Strachey; introduction by Ernst Kris; 218-21. New York:

Basic Books, 1954. Freud's first mention of the Oedipal scene, with reference to his own dreams.

_____. *Totem and Taboo.* In *The Basic Writings of Sigmund Freud*, edited and translated by A. A. Brill, 914-30. New York: Modern Library, 1938. Further development of the Oedipal drama, positing collective parricide as the origin of ethics, guilt, culture, art, and exogamy.

Gimferrer, Pere. "Aproximaciones a Manuel Puig." *Plural* 57 (June 1976): 21-25. Characterization of Puig's enterprise as a criticism of language, with a pronouncedly moral thrust.

Goytisolo, Juan. "On Being Morally Correct." *Review of Contemporary Fiction* 11, no. 3 (1991): 186-88. Eulogizes Puig's writing as courageously out of step with tendency to moral indifference.

Levine, Suzanne Jill. "Manuel Puig Exits Laughing." *Review of Contemporary Fiction* 11, no. 3 (1991): 159-64. (Also appears as "Manuel Puig among the Stars [Exit Laughing]." *World Literature Today* 65, no. 4 [1991]: 587-94.) Privileged glimpse into the translational process and the author's persona provided by Puig's main translator.

Magnarelli, Sharon. "Betrayed by the Cross-Stitch." In *The Lost Rib: Female Characters in the Spanish-American Novel*, 117-46. London and Toronto: Associate University Presses, 1985. Linguistically attuned feminist analysis of Mita's plight in *Betrayed by Rita Hayworth*.

Sarduy, Severo. "Note to the Notes to the Notes . . . A Propos of Manuel Puig." Adapted and translated by Suzanne Jill Levine. *World Literature Today* 65, no. 4 (1991): 625-30. (Originally published in *Revista Iberoamericana* 37 [1971]: 555-67.) Performative appreciation of the kitschy, pastiche, carnivalesque qualities of Puig's writing.

Shaw, Donald L. *Nueva narrativa hispanoamericana.* Madrid: Cátedra, 1983. See pp. 197-201. Locates Puig in the "Boom junior" and judges *Heartbreak Tango* to be the "best structured" of his first four novels.

Southard, David R. "*Betrayed by Rita Hayworth*: Reader Deception and Anti-climax in His Novels." *Latin American Literary Review* 4, no. 9 (1976): 22-28. Formalist and reader-re(de)ception approaches combined.

Yúdice, George. "*El beso de la mujer araña* y *Pubis angelical*: Entre el placer y el saber." In *Literature and Popular Culture in the Hispanic World: A Symposium*, edited by Rose S. Minc, 43-57. Gaithersburg, Md.: Hispamérica, 1981. Lacanian reading of *Kiss of the Spider Woman* and *Pubis Angelical* as (phallic) power versus (feminine) knowing.

Index

149

Reich, Wilhelm, 50
"Relative Humidity 95%," 6, 119,
    121-22
Relativism, 2, 9, 18, 23-24, 27, 50,
    55, 68, 91-92, 93-94, 122,
    125, 126
Religious faith, 109-10, 139n12
Repression, 14, 50, 51-52, 66, 77,
    81-82, 106, 126, 127, 136-
    37n9
Revolution, 53-55, 59, 125
Rodríguez Monegal, Emir, 13, 18

Sadism, 37, 40, 119
"The Sado-Masoch Blues," 119
San Sebastián Film Festival, 5
Seix Barral, 4, 5
Serial romance fiction, , 28, 31-
    32
Sexuality, 3, 27, 33-34, 36-37, 40,
    42-43, 110-11, 124, 136-
    37n9
Solotorevsky, Myrna, 29, 74
Southard, David, 21
Subversion, 2, 26, 41, 43, 47, 51-
    52, 59, 68, 69, 79-80, 89,
    117
Suspended Fictions, 75

Technology, 57, 77, 101-2,
    135n11
Third Reich, 55, 73

Third World, 1, 96
Titles, interpretation of Puig's, 8,
    15, 26-27, 29, 31, 36, 41,
    43, 76, 78, 79, 81, 85, 94,
    97, 111, 124, 129
Tropical Night Falling, 1, 2, 6,
    89, 94-102, 103, 109, 126-
    27, 128

Unamuno, Miguel de, 33
Under a Mantle of Stars, 3, 6,
    103, 104-9
"The Usual Suspects," 6, 119,
    120, 122
Utopianism, 30-31, 62, 62, 71, 77-
    78, 85, 106-7, 109

The Villain's Face, 103, 112-14,
    117, 122
"Vivaldi: A Screenplay," 119,
    120-21, 122

White, Hayden, 62
Writing, 2, 10, 18, 20, 21, 26, 27,
    28, 29, 41, 47, 60, 61, 65,
    66-67, 70, 74, 75, 78, 83-84,
    88, 122, 123, 125-26,
    133n10

Yúdice, George, 71

Zola, Emile, 39

The Author

Jonathan Tittler is a professor of Hispanic studies at Cornell University, where he specializes in Spanish American literature and directs the graduate program in the Department of Romance Studies. He holds a Ph.D. from Cornell University. He was president of the Association of North American Colombianists from 1985 to 1987 and was a Fulbright scholar in Colombia in 1991. He currently serves on the editorial boards of *Diacritics: A Review of Contemporary Theory and Criticism*, *Romance Quarterly*, *Latin American Literary Review*, and *Revista de Estudios Colombianos*.

He is the author of *Narrative Irony in the Contemporary Spanish American Novel*, translated and published in Spanish as *Ironía narrativa en la novela hispanoamericana contemporánea*; the editor of *Violencia y literatura en Colombia*; and the translator of several Spanish-American novels. His articles, book reviews, interviews, and translations have been widely published.